The Option Strategy
Desk Reference

The Option Strategy Desk Reference

An Essential Reference for Option Traders

Russell A. Stultz

BEP BUSINESS EXPERT PRESS

First published in 2019 by
Business Expert Press, LLC
222 East 46th Street, New York, NY 10017
www.businessexpertpress.com

ISBN-13: 978-1-94944-390-5 (paperback)
ISBN-13: 978-1-94944-391-2 (e-book)

Business Expert Press Economics and Public Policy Collection

Collection ISSN: 2163-761X (print)
Collection ISSN: 2163-7628 (electronic)

Cover and interior design by S4Carlisle Publishing Services Private Ltd., Chennai, India

First edition: 2019

10 9 8 7 6 5 4 3 2 1

Printed in the United States of America.

Advanced Quotes for *The Option Strategy Desk Reference*

"Russell Stultz's *The Option Strategy Desk Reference* is a fantastic resource for self-directed investors. As a full-time trader myself, the strategies laid out in the book are commonplace for experienced option traders. Russell has done a great job in dissecting the components of each strategy, as well as providing a plan of action for every possible scenario a strategy may encounter. A helpful graph is accompanied with each strategy to precisely illustrate their risk and reward characteristics.

Drawing on personal experience, seasoned option traders usually create their own strategy reference guides after years of testing what works and what does not. With Russell's book, an amateur trader can avoid much of the painful (and potentially costly) trial-and-error trades in order to achieve success faster. Overall, I would recommend this book to any novice or expert trader looking to expand/reinforce his or her trading toolkit and knowledge base."

—*Michael Marquardt*, CPA, MAcc; Options Trading Instructor; Full-time options trader

"If you want options trading strategies stripped down to their most succinct and useful level, you will find them in *The Option Strategy Desk Reference*. What makes this book so helpful and credible is that Russell Stultz is a successful trader and an outstanding trainer. With the clear, well-organized and complete way he presents each setup, traders can quickly find the information they need without the fluff—it's pure reference, pure step by step.

I have traded options full time for the last 6 years. Like many others, I have "go to" strategies I use day in and day out. But if I want to employ a trade that is specific to a market situation or that I use infrequently, this desk reference is where I go to confirm I've set up the trade correctly.

Equally, this book is a source of new ideas—perfect for those times where your "go to" isn't working or you want to expand your opportunities for new trades.

My bookshelves are filled with the works of authors that taught me option trading. Those books served their purpose. Now what I require is a tool I can grab when I need it and quickly put to work to make my next trade successful. Russ has given me—and now you—that tool."

—*Mark Armstrong*, BS Engineering Management, dual MA Marketing
and Finance, Full-time options trader

"This is a great reference book. I typically use the same strategies over and over again, but this book is fantastic for experimenting with new option strategies beyond my comfort zone. It's nice to have all 78 strategies in one place with consistent descriptions for each.

I particularly like how a risk profile accompanies each strategy. The book exemplifies the old saying, "A picture is worth a thousand words." The graph is a quick way to determine the profit potential and risk exposure for each strategy. In addition, the description of each strategy, goal, management, profit goal, and stop loss are essential additions."

—*Mo Fatemi*, BS in Electronic Engineering, MA in Computer
Engineering; Founder and Option Trading Instructor, *Investors
Business Daily* Meetup, Plano, Texas; Lecturer, North Texas
Investment Strategies Club; Full-time options trader

"*The Option Strategy Desk Reference* by Russell Stultz presents a comprehensive investment study guide to financial options. Mr. Stultz's unique educational and teaching background has brought together a comprehensive, clearly written, and concise approach to options trading. His book provides a truly comprehensive guide for both beginning and seasoned option traders.

As a full-time, experienced option trader myself, I refer to this book when analyzing and executing my trades. I consider it to be an essential reference in my understanding of how options work, especially with the risk graphs that accompany each of the 78 strategies. The book provides the only strategy reference a serious option trader will ever need. I give this book a 5-star rating!"

—*Donald E. Pearson*, MD, Full-time options trader

Abstract

Purpose

This book was created to provide an extensive option trading tutorial in addition to being a convenient and extensive option strategy reference. It includes 78 option strategies. Each strategy includes a corresponding trade example that can be used by both new and experienced option traders. Each strategy example can be adjusted to fit current market values; each can be entered and thoroughly tested through simulation. Only after the reader understands how the strategy works should he or she risk real money on the selected strategy. Therefore, the author strongly recommends trading in simulation to develop a thorough familiarity with the dynamics of each strategy. When a strategy proves to be reliable, it may be added to the reader's repertoire of trading strategies.

Why 78 Option Strategies?

It is rare, if not unlikely, for active option traders to use more than 6 to 10 different option strategies. Among these are the short cash covered put, bull call, bull put, iron condor, and perhaps the long call butterfly. But this is only six. The book includes these 6 and another 72. For example, the synthetic long stock combo, among several others, is just one strategy that should probably be added to every option trader's repertoire of favored strategies. The breadth of the strategies contained within the book is likely to add several more strategy choices from which to choose in order to enhance a trader's skills and income potential.

Using the Strategies

Each strategy within the book includes a trade setup description; risk and reward potential; a sample trade; a corresponding risk profile that plots each trade's profit or loss on the basis of the price movements of the underlying security (stock, ETF, financial index, etc.); trader market bias, that is, bullish, neutral, or bearish; setup parameters including the price trend (upward, neutral, or downward); and one or more typical delta values for strike price selection. The delta values are used to determine the probability of a position becoming in the money or remaining out of the money throughout the life of the corresponding option contracts. The primary goal of each trade is included in addition to trade management techniques, and profit or loss recommendations.

Keywords

finance; income; investing; liquidity; market; options; premium; profit and loss; risk graph; risk management; risk profile; trade management; trading

Contents

Other top-selling option trading classics from the author:

The Only Options Trading Book You'll Ever Need

&

Master 76 Options Strategies

Preface

Every seasoned option trader has several favorite option strategies. They favor these strategies because they know how they work and they almost always return a profit. The specific strategy used is nearly always based on their market bias: bullish—a rallying market, neutral—a sideways market, or bearish—a dropping market. Traders learn how to anticipate rising, neutral, and falling markets by scanning and analyzing price charts, using a handful of chart studies, and checking corresponding buying and selling volumes, something they call *volatility*. Armed with a rational market bias enhances their odds for success. This information is used to select one of their favorite option strategies that is compatible with their market bias.

And knowing precisely how a strategy works leads to rational trade management, that is, when to close the trade for profit, roll the trade to a later option expiration date, convert a failing strategy into a winning one, or perhaps simply close an unsalvageable trade and try something different.

The flexibility available to option traders is both unique and immense. No other trading venue lets an investor "switch horses in the middle of the stream." Moreover, being able to determine the mathematical probabilities or "odds" of achieving a profitable outcome is an advantage that's unavailable to those who just buy and sell stocks, futures, or foreign exchange currency pairs.

If you're already an option trader, this book delivers a useful synopsis of 78 different option strategies. If you want to learn how to "get in the game" and start earning a steady income, then learn what successful option traders know by reading (and applying the option trading rules) I provide in *The Only Options Trading Book You'll Ever Need* available from amazon.com.

Disclaimer

Trading and investing always involve risk. Any money traded or invested can be lost. You alone are responsible for any trading or investing activity that you undertake. Neither the author nor the publisher is licensed, qualified, or authorized to provide trading or investing advice nor will they assume any responsibility for your investment activities. Hence, by reading this disclaimer and the information within this book, you understand that there is always risk involved in trading stocks, exchange traded funds, financial indexes, option contracts, futures, and foreign exchange currency pairs. The author and publisher make no representations or warranties for your trading success nor will they be held liable for your actions.

Acknowledgments

Thanks to the many members of the North Texas Investment Strategies Club who regularly critique option, futures, and forex strategies that are described in the club's monthly investment and trading strategy presentations. In particular, I wish to thank long-time, professional option traders and instructors Mo Fatemi, Mark Armstrong, and Michael Marquardt. My thanks to Dr. Donald Pearson, MD, who became an active options trader after reading the first draft of my first options book. Don used my trading rules and setups, chose several strategies, and proved the value of my book within a matter of weeks. Thank you, Don!

Introduction

Why We Trade Options

Option trading is quite likely the fastest growing investment venue in the world. If it isn't, it certainly should be. There are many good reasons for its explosive popularity. First, many individual option traders earn more income from trading options than they earn from their full-time jobs. Many who retire from their job careers and learn the nuances of option trading quickly discover they can earn more income trading options by spending 1 or 2 hours a day than they did working every week day from 8:00 a.m. till 5:00 p.m. And they don't have to make that daily round trip to the office, pay tolls and parking fees, or fight traffic. At least, that's been my personal experience and that of many people I personally know who have learned how to earn steady incomes trading options.

And learning how to enter, manage, and close option trades for profit is not "rocket science." It's simple arithmetic. The beauty of options is that they are mathematically predictable. Option traders quickly learn how to use statistical probabilities to manage their trading outcomes. And their odds are much better than those of a gambling casino. Casinos thrive on 54.5 percent odds of winning over their client gamblers, who are left with 44.5 percent odds of winning. If gamblers stay at the tables long enough, they will lose their entire bankroll to the casino. But option traders learn how to structure their option trades to achieve winning odds at or even greater than 70 percent and some strategies that exceed 9.5:1 odds of winning.

Of course, before you can benefit from these impressive option trading odds, you must

1. understand how options work.
2. open and fund an account with a reputable brokerage.
3. learn to use your brokerage's trading software.

4. develop a set of options trading rules.

5. learn to use a handful of options strategies.

6. apply your rules to your daily trading and options management tasks.

Option Education and Books

There are many options books you can read, but I recommend *The Only Options Trading Book You'll Ever Need*. I wrote that book for people who want to learn how to analyze price charts and trade options from scratch. These people may want to supplement the income provided by their day jobs, or they may be retired, on social security, and have a stagnant 401K or individual retirement account (IRA). They would benefit from an alternate income source. Those stagnant retirement funds can be converted to rollover IRAs with any reputable brokerage and their values multiplied by trading them. Many option traders have doubled and even quadrupled the value of their qualified retirement accounts. If they can do it, you can do it too.

I wrote the above-mentioned option trading book for people who do not know how the market works but who want to learn. This is important, regardless of what kind of trader you are—from a buy-and-wish stock investor to one who invests in commodity futures. My book goes through the entire process. The following is a partial list of the topics covered:

- Choosing a brokerage
- Funds transfer
- Negotiating commissions and trading fees
- Selecting and setting up trading equipment
- Installing essential communication devices
- Developing backup systems
- Analyzing price charts
- Using chart studies to determine current supply and demand

- Understanding and using *Option Chains*
- Learning option math (called the *Greeks*)
- Understanding the impact of volatility, liquidity, and the passage of time on option values
- Developing a set of sound, fact-based option trading rules to enhance trading outcomes
- Understanding how to set up, enter, and manage a broad range of option strategies
- Learning how to measure trade probabilities
- Knowing how to manage risk
- Developing and scanning a watch list of trade candidates, that is, stocks, exchange-traded funds (ETFs), financial indexes, and futures
- Mastering the use and management of several option strategies
- Closing trades for profits
- Rolling trades up, out, and/or down
- Legging a failing trade strategy into a winning trade strategy
- Trading small brokerage accounts and rollover IRAs.

The above-mentioned topics, and many others, may seem daunting. But they are not that complex. And if you have my book, you can "own the knowledge," because the carefully crafted glossary and alphabetical index guide you to essential information in a flash.

Option Premium—Insurance policy sellers collect premium from insurance policy buyers. Insurance companies sell their policy holders options. These premiums lose value with time and expire worthless when the insurance policy expires. But, if you suffer a loss on your insured property while the insurance policy is in force, you can "exercise your option" to collect insurance for that loss. Like the insurance policy, options are a depreciating asset. Premium value exits each and every day until the option contract expires worthless.

Just for review, a typical option chain is included on the following page.

MSFT   MICROSOFT CORP COM 108.27 ETB NASDAQ

✓ Underlying

>	Last X	Net Chng	Bid X	Ask X
	108.27 Y	-.73	108.27 Q	108.28 Z

CALLS

Mark	Delta	Gamma	Theta	Vega	Open Int	Bid X	Ask X	Strike
✓ 14 SEP 18	(32)	100 (Weeklys)						
6.300	1.00	.00	.00	.32	36	5.85 M	6.75 M	102
5.750	.85	.04	-.02	.08	211	5.70 M	5.80 C	103
4.925		IN THE MONEY (ITM) CALL OPTIONS			5	4.90 H	4.95 N	104
4.150	.74	.08	-.03	.10	86	4.10 H	4.20 M	105
3.450	.68	.07	-.03	.12	125	3.40 M	3.50 C	106
2.800	.61	.07	-.03	.12	320	2.77 H	2.83 H	107
2.340 (AT THE MONEY STRIKE)	.53	.08	-.03	.13	138	2.22 N	2.26 H	108
1.750	.46	.08	-.03	.13	159	1.73 M	1.77 Z	109
1.350	.38	.07	-.03	.12	1,418	1.33 N	1.37 Z	110
1.010	.31	.07	-.03	.12	87	99 N	1.03 H	111
.745		OUT OF THE MONEY (OTM) CALL OPTIONS				.73 N	.76 Z	112
.540	.19	.05	-.02	.09	83	52 N	.56 Z	113
.380	.15	.04	-.02	.07	42	36 M	.40 H	114
.270	.11	.04	-.01	.06	114	26 H	.28 Q	115
> 21 SEP 18	(39)	100						

Figure 1 The call half of an option chain

MSFT   MICROSOFT CORP COM 108.27 ETB NASDAQ

✓ Underlying

>	Last X	Net Chng	Bid X	Ask X
	108.27 Y	-.73	108.27 Q	108.28 Z

PUTS

Strike	Bid X	Ask X	Mark	Delta	Gamma	Theta	Vega	Open Int
✓ 14 SEP 18	(32)	100 (Weeklys)						17.91% (±4.646)
102	.51 H	.54 H	.525	-.15	.04	-.02	.08	1,230
103	.68 H	.69 M	.675	-.19	.04	-.03	.09	826
104	.83 H	.87 M	.850	-.23	.05	-.03	.10	165
105	1.06 H	1.09 H	OUT OF THE MONEY (OTM) PUT OPTIONS					241
106	1.35 N	1.38 H	1.365	-.34	.06	-.03	.12	87
107	1.70 H	1.74 H	1.720	-.40	.07	-.03	.13	60
108	2.14 N	2.18 M	2.160	-.47	.07	(AT THE MONEY STRIKE)		
109	2.65 N	2.69 Q	2.670	-.54	.07	-.03	.13	125
110	3.25 M	3.30 M	3.275	-.60	.07	-.03	.13	52
111	3.85 M	4.05 H	3.950	-.66	.06	-.03	.12	0
112	4.65 C	4.75 M	IN THE MONEY (ITM) PUT OPTIONS				.11	67
113	5.45 M	5.65 M	5.550	-.76	.05	-.03	.10	10
114	6.30 M	6.45 M	6.375	-.80	.04	-.03	.09	1
115	5.70 M	8.75 M	7.225	-.83	.04	-.02	.08	6
> 21 SEP 18	(39)	100						20.02% (±5.723)

Figure 2 The put half of an option chain

Using Option Chain Values

NOTE: Delta, Gamma, Theta, Rho, and Vega (although Vega is not in the Greek alphabet) are commonly referred to as the *option Greeks*. These *Greek* values are displayed in the columns of option chains for each *strike* price. Experienced option traders examine these as part of their trading analysis. The *Rho* Greek (rate of interest) is significant only when interest rates are high, so Rho is rarely displayed for analysis purposes when interest rates are low and reasonably stable.

High interest rates increase call premiums; when Rho is low, put premiums are typically higher than call premiums. Other values can also be displayed, such as *Extrinsic Value, Intrinsic Value, Last,* and so on. However, displaying too many columns on an option chain creates clutter and makes it difficult to read.

Premium (MARK)—Option traders search for sufficient premium values displayed in the Mark column to justify the risks involved in their trades. The Mark value is typically midway between the Bid and Ask column values. Narrow bid-to-ask widths indicate strong trading volume and liquidity. This is also reflected by each strike's Open Interest value described in the following paragraphs. When wide, the Mark moves within a much wider price range, referred to as "slippage."

Some consider premium values of 30 cents or higher to be acceptable, especially when an extremely high probability of success exists. When premium is insufficient, continue scanning your list of trading candidates (your watch list) and the underlying price charts. Find imbalances in supply and demand near support or resistance. Study the price trend and develop a rational trading bias. Check the implied volatility (IV percent) at the top of the option chain; the average 14-day price move, that is, the ATR(14) study; the times till expiration; and an oversold/overbought momentum study such as the moving average convergence divergence (MACD) or relative strength index (RSI). Examine the option values including the Greeks, alluded to in the following paragraphs, Open Interest, and sufficient premium to warrant each trade's risk.

Delta—Delta and Gamma relate directly to premium values (option prices) of the underlying security; the Mark (market price) is the midpoint between the Bid and the Ask. Delta measures the option premium's sensitivity to a $1.00 change in the value of the underlying security. Although many believe that a Delta value of 0.45 causes the premium to change by 45 cents for a $1.00 change in the underlying security, it's more complicated. The impact of Delta on option premium values uses a complex formula with several variables, such as Lambda and Psi, which are not shown on option chains. But it's easy to examine Delta values at different strike prices on any option chain. Delta values are positive for long calls and negative for long puts. Delta values are negative for short calls and positive for short puts. Moving from low to high strike prices, call Deltas range from 1.00 to 0.00; put Deltas range from 0.00 to −1.00.

Gamma—Gamma calculates how much the value of Delta changes for each $1.00 change in the underlying. If a 0.40 Delta of a long call has a Gamma of 0.05, a $1.00 drop in the price of the underlying security reduces the value of the call's Delta to 0.35. A $1.00 rally in the price of the underlying security would increase the call's Delta value from 0.40 to 0.45. Gamma is highest "at the money" (ATM) (the strike nearest the price of the underlying security—stock, ETF, and so on) and declines in value at strike prices either deeper in the money (ITM) or farther out of the money (OTM). This incrementally reduces the amount Delta changes as it moves away from "the money" in either direction. This sluggishness is an incentive to close a trade once the effect of Gamma on Delta offsets a trade's benefit from price movement in the underlying optioned security.

Theta—Theta measures the effect of the passage of each day in time on an option's premium (Mark) value. Theta increases as an option approaches its expiration date and ultimately reduces premium to 0 at option expiration. A Theta value of 0.05 indicates a reduction in option premium of 5 cents per share per day, or $5.00 per day per 100-share option contract. Without some unforeseen price breakout, it follows that Theta increases in value each day as an option contract approaches expiration. A high Theta value is the enemy of option buyers and the friend of option sellers. Theta can be at 0.00 for long-term (LEAPS) option trades. Having 0 to extremely low Theta values is beneficial to the buyers of LEAPS call options who favor a long-term price increase in the underlying optioned security.

Vega—This "Greek" is sensitive to trading volatility in the underlying security. Option premiums are most responsive to changes in volatility, so Vega has the most impact on option premium values. A Vega value of 0.09 causes the corresponding premium to change by 9 cents per share for each 1.0 percent change in current volatility (IV percent). Using 0.09 Vega, if a premium is presently 30 cents per share, a 3 percent rise in volatility moves the premium value from 30 cents to 57 cents per share [$0.30 + (3 × $0.09) = $0.57] per share, a rise in premium from $30 to $57 per option contract. This is a 90 percent increase in premium resulting from a 3 percent increase in volatility! (Some traders use IV Rank, which is a percentage of the past 12 months' volatility, called "historical volatility." While IV percent can range beyond 100 percent, IV Rank values remain between 0 and 100.

Open Interest—The Open Interest tells option traders how many option contracts are currently open at each strike price. This is a measure of option liquidity and therefore is extremely important. Insufficient liquidity makes it difficult to enter or exit an option trade. Always look for a few hundred working contracts at the strike prices of interest. Also calculate the total number of open option contracts for all calls and puts that exist on the selected option chain. Having a large number of working trades makes trade entries and exits much more responsive.

Using Risk Profiles

Every option trading platform can display a *risk profile*, also called a *risk graph*. Regardless of what we call it, the risk profile displays a graphical plot that shows traders how each option trade responds to changes in the price of the underlying security.

The following are two risk graph illustrations and a snapshot of the Probability Analysis display for the same bull put spread strategy. The bull put option strategy is described later in this book.

Figure 3 shows an option trade entered on July 28, 2017. This trade sells 10 $143 QQQ puts and buys 10 $140 QQQ puts. The order bars at the bottom of the figure show a credit of $0.75 cents per share for a total

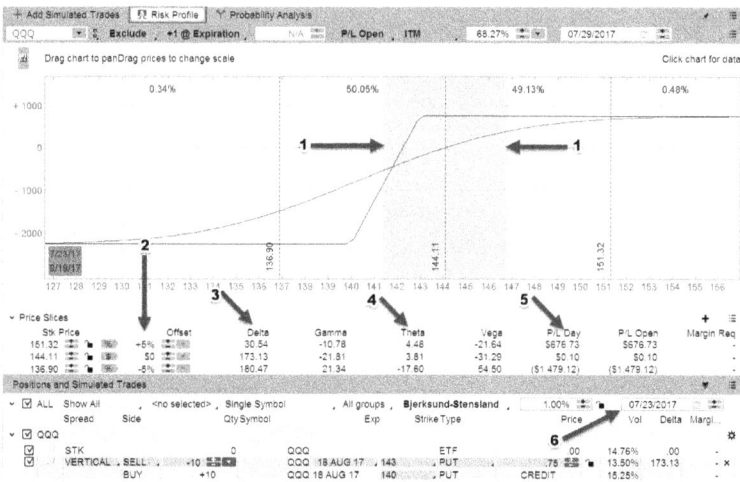

Figure 3 Example of a risk profile

For illustration purposes only.

credit of $750 in option premium. Recall how the term *short* is used when selling and *long* is used when buying stocks, options, and futures. These terms are used throughout this book.

Notice the vertical dashed line at $144.11 on the X axis. This is the current price of the underlying QQQ NASDAQ 100 ETF. The gray shaded area (#1) on either side of the vertical $144.11 line represents 1 standard deviation (68.27 percent) above and below the current price of QQQ. The smooth line represents the calculated *hypothetical price* of the underlying equity. This plot is based on the underlying math, which in this case is based on the trending price of the QQQ ETF.

Option traders often use 1 standard deviation as a measure of probability. This value is derived from current trading volume. The math indicates that QQQ prices that exist above and below 1 standard deviation have a 67.28 percent likelihood of being OTM when the selected QQQ option contracts expire on August 18, 2017. More conservative traders move even farther OTM. For example, call Delta values at or less than 0.25 and put Delta values at or greater than −0.25 are common.

The Price Slices (#2) are used to estimate profits or losses at different prices of the underlying security. Price slices are adjustable in dollars, percentage, or by standard deviation, represented by the Greek letter σ (sigma).

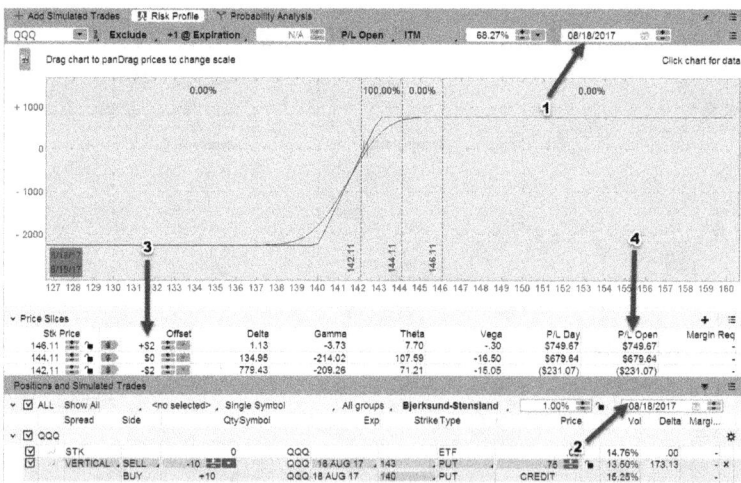

Figure 4 Risk profile, dates (#1 and #2) and price slices (#3) adjusted

For illustration purposes only.

The Greeks, including Delta (#3) Gamma, Theta (#4), and Vega, plus the profit or loss (P/L) Day (#5) and P/L Open, are also shown. As an options trader, you know how Theta represents the daily reduction in the value of long option premium. Delta shows us how the premium value changes relative to a $1.00 increase or decrease in the price of the optioned security—the Powershares QQQ ETF in the example.

Figure 4 illustrates how price slices (#3) can been adjusted by $2.00 above and $2.00 below the current price of QQQ—the center price slice. Vertical dashed lines that correspond to your price slice values are added to the graph. Looking across the +$2 price slice at the P/L Open (#4), a $2.00 increase in QQQ's price returns a $749.67 profit. You can also add more price slices above and below to see the Greek and P/L values at different hypothetical price levels.

Figure 5 illustrates the Probability Analysis. The Powershares QQQ ETF prices inside the cone-shaped plot include those QQQ prices that remain within the 68.27 percent standard deviation value. Prices above and below the cone-shaped envelope have a 68.27 percent statistical probability of being OTM at contract expiration.

You can adjust the value of the **Prob. range** to test other values, such as 75 percent or 80 percent. You can also select 2 standard deviations (95.45 percent), which are also used by some option traders—especially on high-priced stocks and financial indexes with high option premium

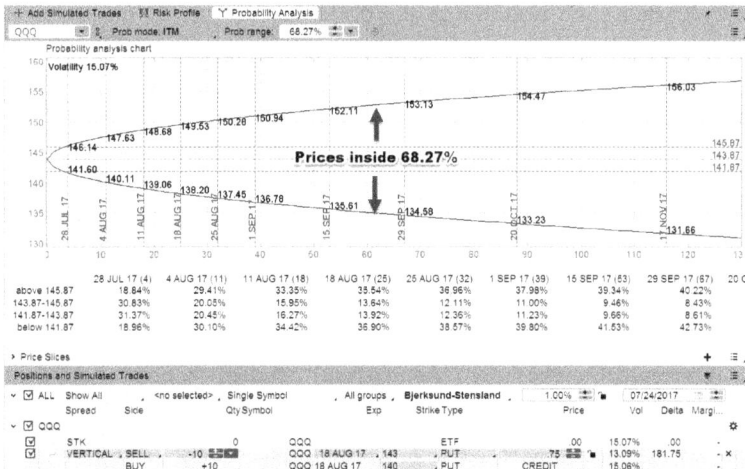

Figure 5 The probability analysis For illustration purposes only.

values. The default setting of the **Prob. mode** is **ITM**. You can change this setting to **OTM** or the more conservative **Touching** on the basis of your personal preference. The Probability of Touching values is typically within a few percentage points of being two times the value of Delta. In contrast to being OTM at expiration, the Probability of Touching value assumes that the corresponding strike price will never *touch* the ATM strike price throughout the duration of the trade. However, even math is never 100 percent reliable.

Rules-Based Trading

Trading rules are used by those who trade as a business. Without rules, it's difficult to know why trades aren't working, particularly if they are entered helter-skelter and are constantly failing. So, here's a starting place:

Time—Sell options that expire inside 7 weeks (56 days). Always choose the nearest expiration date possible that is consistent with acceptable premium values. Buy options that remain in force for 90 days or more. Having more time reduces the daily reduction in option premium, measured by the value of the option Greek Theta.

Probability—When selling options to collect option premium, select strike prices that are far OTM with call Delta values of 0.25 or less and put Delta values of −0.25 or higher. (To clarify, a Delta value of −0.10 is *higher* than a put Delta value of −0.25.)

Volatility—Buy options when current implied volatility is low and premium values are relatively inexpensive. Sell options when volatility is high and premium values are high. Traders count on implied volatility to return to historical levels. Consider adding IV Rank to your price charts.

ATR(14) in dollars and percent—Always check the recent price movement in both dollar and percentage terms. Although useful, these values are based on history. The random nature of the market can "turn on a dime."

Oversold/Overbought (Momentum) Studies—Check these studies for the current buying or selling momentum. Exceptionally high or low values indicate overbought or oversold, respectively. Look for all four study values to be in agreement for confidence.

Premium—An acceptable premium value depends on each trader's personal goals and risk tolerance. How much do you want to earn? How much are you willing to risk? What must you pay in commissions and option exchange fees to make a trade worthwhile? Once you determine the answers to these questions, you may be able to select a minimum premium amount. Setting a minimum premium value simplifies trading. If your rule is a minimum of $0.30 in premium per 100-share option contract, then your trade scanning becomes easier. You can discard all trades that do not meet your minimum premium requirement within a few seconds.

Open Interest—This is a measure of liquidity. When liquidity is good, orders fill rapidly, making both entry and exit faster. As a "rule of thumb," many traders look for Open Interest values of 300 or more at the strike price of interest. This is especially true when trading a large number of option contracts. Others settle for Open Interest values that are 10 times the number of contracts traded. Using this rule, a 5-contract order would require an Open Interest value of at least 50, (5 × 10 = 50). *Always* look at Open Interest values above and below on both the call and put sides of the option chain to verify ample trading volume exists on the selected option chain.

When using 3- or 4-strike option strategies, seek Open Interest of 300 or more. When using a 1- to 2- strike option strategy, 10× the number of options may work. But to be filled quickly, your premium must be fairly priced. And be mindful that it's much more important to close a trade for profit or to prevent a loss than to open a trade for speculation. Do what is necessary to exit quickly for profit or to avoid an unwanted loss. Many seasoned traders will give up five cents in premium to fill an open order.

Risk Tolerance—How much money are you willing to lose? Each strategy has a potential risk and reward. The size of your trade governs how much money is put at risk. Many traders use the total marginable equity held in their brokerage accounts to govern the amount they're willing to risk. For example, if they are willing to lose 1.0 percent of a $25,000 account, they would never risk more than $250 on a single trade. This illustrates how it takes money to make money. An unwillingness to lose more than $250 in a trade makes it difficult to grow an account. However, by simultaneously keeping half-a-dozen high-probability trades working, traders can ensure that their account can achieve rapid growth. And options provide traders with a number of *defined-risk* option strategies, such as iron condors, bull put spreads, and butterflies. These, and many others, limit the total amount of money that can possibly be lost. Others, like the synthetic long stock strategy, can return a substantial amount of money for a small investment. But, of course, the trader's bullish bias must be correct. Be sure to study these strategies. Try them in simulation to see how they can be put to work for a steady income.

Using the Strategies

Within the 78 strategies included in the remainder of this book, the number of 100-share option contracts, designated by *n*, is provided in the setups for each strategy. A brief description of each follows.

Bias, Risk, Reward: Each strategy is accompanied by a trader's bias, that is, bullish (uptrending price), bearish (downtrending price), neutral (sideways moving "stuck" price). The risk and reward indicators correspond to each strategy's outcome potential for profits and/or losses. Many traders specialize in selling options for premium income. These are considered "low-reward" strategies, although many option traders make tens of thousands of dollars in weekly incomes by selling put and call options and vertical put and call "spreads," such as the short put and the bull put and bull call strategies described in this book.

Price Charts: Option traders analyze price charts to determine price support and resistance levels. These correspond to demand and supply. When a stock is oversold, the price drops, which attracts buyers. When overbought, the price drops from selling activity. Therefore, be sure to examine price charts to see where the price has been and to determine what is most likely to occur relative to buying or selling.

Delta is used by option traders to gauge the statistical probability of an option price to become ITM prior to the option's contract expiration date. Many option traders use Delta 0.25 as a 25 percent likelihood of the corresponding option's strike price becoming ITM prior to expiration.

Implied Volatility (IV percent) is used by option traders for strategy selection. When IV percent (or IV Rank) is high, premiums are high. This encourages option traders to choose a strategy that sells premium. The seller is rewarded when the premium begins to decline in value, which permits the seller to buy to close the option contract for substantially less premium than originally received, that is, sell for a dollar, buy back for 25 cents—a profit of 75 cents per share. When IV percent is low, premiums are low. This encourages the use of option strategies that buy premium. The buyer may buy for $0.25 per share and sell for $1.00 per share—a 400 percent profit.

Glossary

A glossary of option terms and definitions is included at the end of this book. If you encounter an unfamiliar term or abbreviation, be sure to check the glossary for a definition. For a complete options tutorial that takes its readers from basic concepts to advanced topics, including technical analysis, rules-based options trading, trading options on futures, trading options on small accounts, and much more, see *The Only Options Trading Book You'll Ever Need*, which is available from Amazon in both paperback and Kindle formats.

Short Call

Strategy: Sell *n* OTM Calls, ≤ 56 days till expiration (DTE)

Example:

Strategy	Buy/ Sell	Qty	Symbol	Trade Date	Expiration Date	Strike	Type	Price
Short Call	SELL	−10	ALKS	7/19/17	8/18/17	$65	CALL	$0.68

Bias: Neutral to Bearish * Risk: High * Reward: High

Short Call Risk Profile

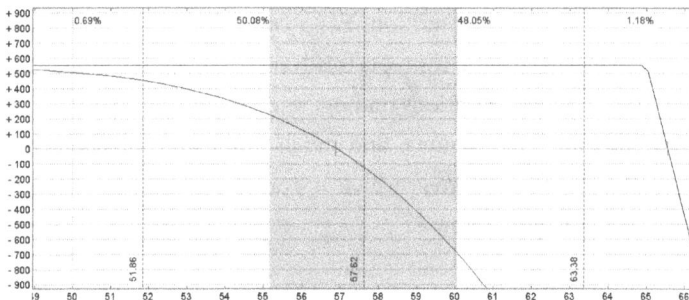

Price Chart: Downtrending or moving sideways

Current IV%: ≥ 60%

IV Rank: ≥ 60

Trade: Sell one or more OTM call options.

Strike Delta: ≤ −0.25 (75% Probability OTM)

Goals: Sell far OTM calls for premium income on a neutral to down-trending security. Let Theta reduce the premium until the short calls can be closed for a fraction of the premium originally received.

This is an uncovered (or "naked") short call. Only traders who are granted the highest option trading level by their brokerage can trade uncovered short calls. This applies to several strategies such as the covered call, bull call, diagonal bull call, etc.

Manage: If the short calls remain safely OTM, either close them for profit when time value reduces its premium or let them expire worthless. If the price of the underlying begins to rally, close the trade to prevent the short call from becoming ITM.

Profit: Close when this trade returns a profit of 30 percent or more.

Loss: Close when this trade approaches an 8 percent loss.

Long Call

Strategy: Buy *n* Calls, ≥ 90 DTE

Example:

Strategy	Buy/ Sell	Qty	Symbol	Trade Date	Exp. Date	Strike	Type	Price
Long Call	BUY	+2	FB	7/19/17	10/20/17	$165.00	CALL	$7.85

Bias: Bullish * Risk: Low * Reward: High

Long Call Risk Profile

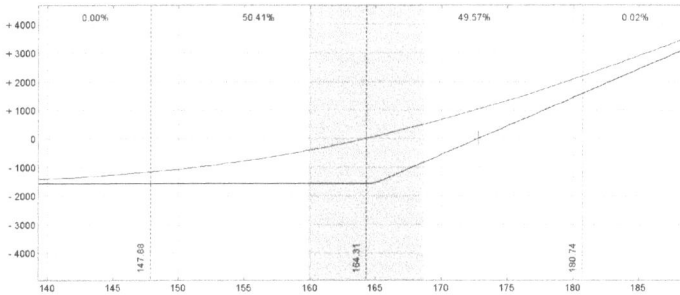

Price Chart: Uptrending

Current IV%: ≤ 20%

IV Rank: ≤ 30

Trade: Buy one or more ATM or slightly ITM or OTM call options.

Strike Delta: ≥ 0.55

Goals: Buy one or more call options on an underlying security that is trending upward. Provide ample time for the long calls to move ITM for a corresponding increase in premium value. Long options are purchased for a fraction of the stock price. If the price of the underlying continues to rally, the return on investment is substantially better than a similar trade made on the underlying stock or ETF itself.

Manage: If the long call has returned an acceptable profit, and before Theta begins to erode its premium value, close the long calls for profit.

If deep ITM, determine if exercising the option (receiving the intrinsic value less the remaining extrinsic value) is more profitable than simply selling the long call options for the current premium value.

Profit: Close when this trade returns a profit of 30 percent or more.

Loss: Close this trade if the price of the underlying reverses direction as a result of poor earnings or an unexpected corporate or financial sector event and the remaining premium approaches a 10 percent reduction in value.

Short Put

Strategy: Sell *n* OTM Puts, Expire ≤ 56 DTE

Example:

Strategy	Buy/Sell	Qty	Symbol	Trade Date	Exp. Date	Strike	Type	Price
Short Put	SELL	−3	ACAD	5/20/17	6/16/17	$25.00	PUT	$0.60

Bias: Bullish or Neutral * Risk: Moderate to Low * Reward: Moderate to High

Short Put Risk Profile

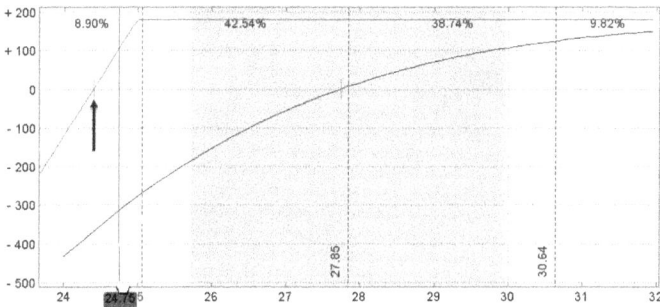

Price Chart: Uptrending or moving sideways

Current IV%: ≥ 60%

IV Rank: ≥ 70

Trade: Sell one or more OTM put options.

Typical Strike Delta: ≤ 0.25 (75% Probability OTM)

Goals: Sell a far OTM put for premium income on a neutral to uptrending security. Let Theta reduce the premium until the short puts can be purchased for a fraction of the amount of premium originally received. This strategy is also referred to as a cash-covered put.

Manage: If the short put remains safely OTM, either close it for profit when time value reduces its premium or let it expire worthless. If the price of the underlying begins to rally, close the trade to prevent the short put from becoming ITM.

Profit: Close when this trade returns a profit of 30 percent or more.

Loss: Close when this trade approaches an 8 percent loss.

Long Put

Strategy: Buy n Puts, Expire ≥ 90 DTE

Example:

Strategy	Buy/ Sell	Qty	Symbol	Trade Date	Exp. Date	Strike	Type	Price
Long Put	BUY	+3	ATVI	5/22/17	8/18/17	$55.00	PUT	−$2.40

Bias: Bearish * Risk: Low * Reward: High

Long Put Risk Profile

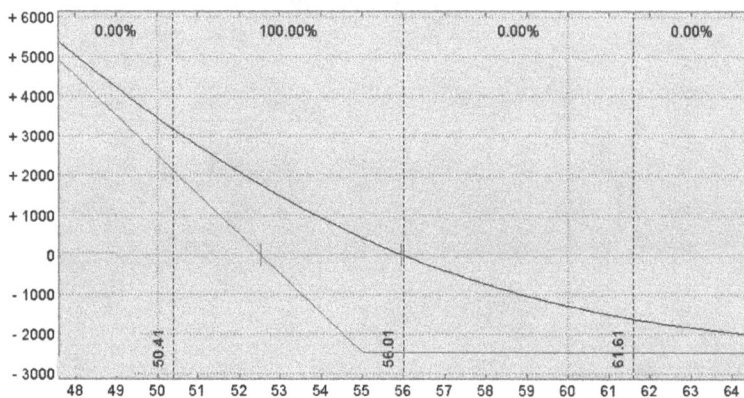

Price Chart: Downtrending

Current IV%: ≤ 25%

IV Rank: ≤ 30

Trade: Buy one or more put options.

Typical Strike Delta: ≥ −0.45 to −0.55

Goals: A strong drop in the price of the underlying is required to move the long put deeper ITM, which increases premium value.

Manage: If the long put moves deeper ITM according to the trader's bearish bias, it is sold for substantially more premium than originally paid. If the price of the underlying begins to rally, sell the long put and consider buying a long call to take advantage of the price increase.

Profit: Close when this trade returns a profit of 30 percent or more.

Loss: Close when this trade approaches an 8 percent loss.

Covered Call

Strategy: Buy n Calls, ≥ 90 DTE
Buy or Own n × 100 Shares

Example:

Strategy	Buy/Sell	Qty	Symbol	Trade Date	Exp. Date	Strike	Type	Price
Covered Call	BUY/OWN	+1,000	EXAS				STOCK	−$30.01
	SELL	−10	EXAS	5/22/17	6/16/17	$35.00	CALL	$0.35

Bias: Bullish * Risk: Low * Reward: Low

Covered Call Risk Profile

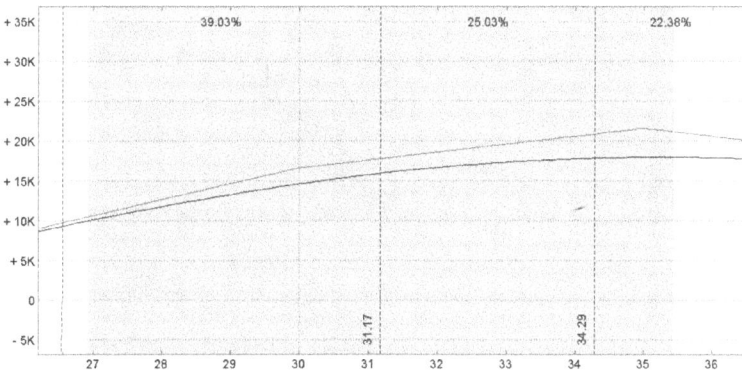

Price Chart: Uptrending or moving sideways

Current IV%: ≥ 60%

IV Rank: ≥ 70

Trade: Sell one OTM call option for each 100 "covering" shares held within the trader's brokerage account.

Typical Strike Delta: ≤ −0.40 (≈ 60% Probability OTM)

Goals: A strong rally in the price of the underlying required to move the long call deeper ITM to increase premium value; collect premium from the short call to partially offset the premium paid when this trade is entered.

Manage: If the stock rallies and increases in value, be prepared to close the long stock for profit and the short calls to prevent them from becoming ITM. If the price of the underlying drops, consider selling the long stock to prevent a major loss. Without the highest trading permission, the trader is required to simultaneously buy to close the short calls. Otherwise, let the short calls expire worthless.

Profit: Close when this trade returns a profit of 30 percent or more.

Loss: Close when this trade approaches an 8 percent loss.

Bull Call

Strategy: Buy n Calls,
Sell n Calls @ Higher Strike
(Same Expiry ≤ 56 DTE)

Example:

Strategy	Buy/ Sell	Qty	Symbol	Trade Date	Exp. Date	Strike	Type	Price
Bull Call	BUY	+5	FB	7/14/17	8/11/17	$160.00	CALL	−$4.73
	SELL	−5	FB	7/14/17	8/11/17	$165.00	CALL	$2.53

Bias: Bullish * Risk: Low * Reward: Low

Bull Call Risk Profile

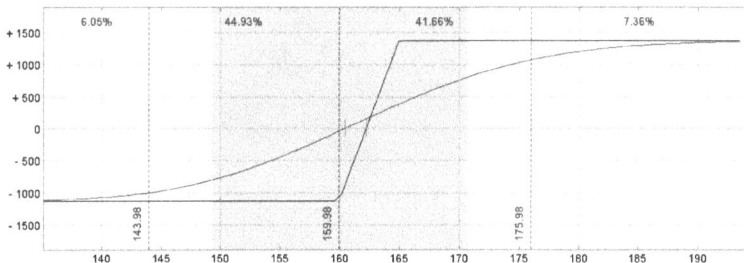

Price Chart: Uptrending

Current IV%: ≤ 20%

IV Rank: ≤ 30

Trade: Buy n call options; sell n call options higher strike.

Typical Strike Deltas:

  Long Call ≈ 0.50 to 0.45*

  Short Call ≤ −0.25 based upon premium

Goals: A strong rally in the price of the underlying required to move the long call deeper ITM to increase premium value; collect premium from the short call to partially offset the premium paid when this trade is entered.

---

*Always consider the calendar or diagonal bull call spreads (both described later in this strategy guide) by using a later expiration date for the long calls.

Manage: If the stock rallies and the long call moves deeper ITM, be prepared to close both the long and short calls for profit. If the price of the underlying drops, sell both the long and short calls. If the highest option trading level is held, the short call may be retained until it expires worthless.

Profit: Close when this trade returns a profit that is greater than or equal to 30 percent.

Loss: Close when this trade approaches an 8 percent loss.

Bull Put

Strategy: Sell *n* Puts,
Buy *n* Puts @ Lower Strike
(Same Expiry ≤ 56 DTE)

Example:

Strategy	Buy/ Sell	Qty	Symbol	Trade Date	Exp. Date	Strike	Type	Price
Bull Put	SELL	−5	FB	5/22/17	8/18/17	$160.00	PUT	$4.73
	BUY	+5	FB	5/22/17	8/18/17	$155.00	PUT	−$2.73

Bias: Bullish * Risk: Low * Reward: Low

Bull Put Risk Profile

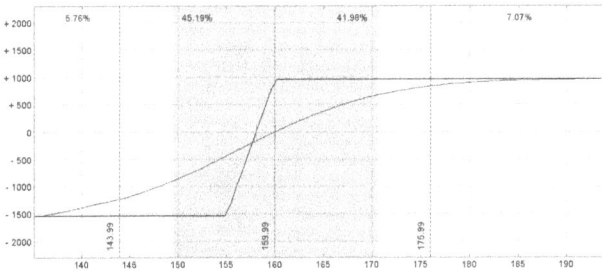

Price Chart: Uptrending

Current IV%: ≥ 60%

IV Rank: ≥ 70

Trade: Sell *n put* options; buy *n put* options lower strike.

Typical Strike Deltas:

Short Put ≥ 0.30 to 0.15

Long Put ≈ 2 to 5 strikes lower; based upon strike widths and premium (greater spread width increases risk)

Goals: Collect more premium from the OTM short put than paid for the farther OTM long put.

Manage: If the short put remains OTM, either let it expire worthless or close the trade for profit. If the underlying drops and threatens the short put, close the trade to prevent the short put from either being ITM at expiration or being exercised.

Profit: Close when this trade returns a profit of 30 percent or more.

Loss: Close when this trade approaches an 8 percent loss.

Horizontal Bull Call Diagonal
Strategy: Sell n ATM Calls, ≤ 56 DTE;
Buy n ATM Calls, Later Expiry

Example:

Strategy	Buy/ Sell	Qty	Symbol	Trade Date	Exp. Date	Strike	Type	Price
Bear Call	SELL	−5	BIDU	12/14/17	12/22/17	$185.00	CALL	$7.15
	BUY	+5	BIDU	12/14/17	12/29/17	$185.00	CALL	−$7.75

Bias: Bullish * Risk: Low * Reward: Low

Horizontal Bull Call Diagonal Risk Profile

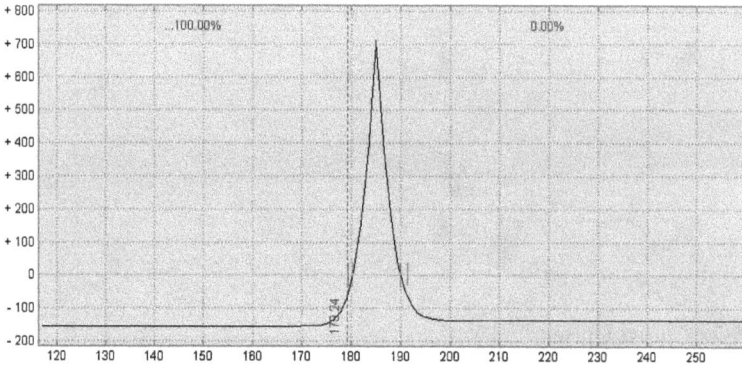

Price Chart: Uptrending

Current IV%: ≤ 20%

IV Rank: ≤ 30

Trade: Sell *n* ATM call options; Buy *n* ATM call options one expiration later.

Typical Strike Deltas:

  Long Call ≈ 0.50 (ATM)

  Short Call ≈ −0.50 (ATM) shorter expiration

Goals: Theta reduces the premium of short call faster than the premium of the long call. Trade may be closed for profit within 1 or 2 days to 1 week.

Manage: As soon as the net premium increases, close the trade for profit. If the underlying rallies, close the trade as the premium of the long call increases faster than the premium of the short call loses premium value.

Profit: Close when profit is at or more than 30 percent (price near peak of witch's hat).

Loss: Close for an 8 percent loss (in case of a price drop).

Bear Put Vertical

Strategy: Sell *n* Puts, ≤ 56 DTE

Buy *n* Puts Higher Strike, Same Expiry

Example:

Strategy	Buy/ Sell	Qty	Symbol	Trade Date	Exp. Date	Strike	Type	Price
Bear Put	SELL	−5	GE	5/26/17	6/23/17	$25.50	PUT	$0.09
	BUY	+5	GE	5/26/17	6/23/17	$27.00	PUT	−$0.42

Bias: Bearish * Risk: Low * Reward: Low

Bear Put Vertical Risk Profile

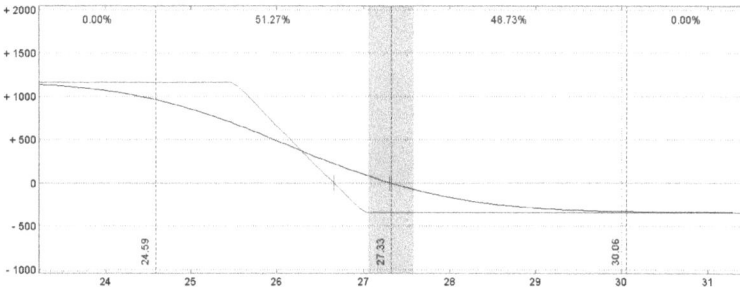

Price Chart: Downtrending

Current IV%: ≤ 25%

IV Rank: ≤ 30%

Trade: Buy *n put* options; sell *n put* options lower strike.

Typical Strike Deltas:

   Long Put ≈ −0.55 to −0.35

   Short Put ≈ 0.25 (should be outside 1 standard deviation).

Goals: Strong price drop that moves long puts deeper ITM for profit; premium from OTM short puts used to reduce entry cost.

Manage: If possible, roll short calls once. Otherwise, close the trade or let it expire worthless.

Profit: Close when profit is at or more than 30 percent.

Loss: Close for an 8 percent loss.

Calendar Bull Call

Strategy: Sell *n* Calls, Expire ≤ 56 DTE

Buy *n* Calls, Lower Strike, One Expiry Later

Example:

Strategy	Buy/Sell	Qty	Symbol	Trade Date	Exp. Date	Strike	Type	Price
Calendar	SELL	−10	AAPL	8/23/17	09/08/17	$165.00	CALL	$0.86
Bull Call	BUY	+10	AAPL	8/23/17	09/15/17	$162.50	CALL	−$2.49

Bias: Bullish * Risk: Low * Reward: Moderate to Low

Calendar Bull Call Risk Profile

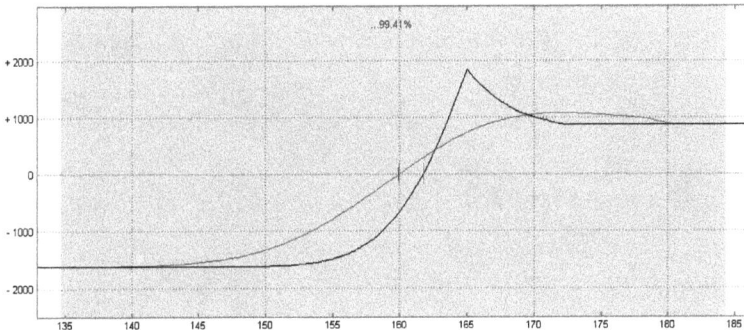

Price Chart: Uptrending

Current IV%: ≤ 20%

IV Rank: ≤ 30

Trade: Buy *n* call options, one expiration later; sell *n* call options, higher strike.

Typical Strike Deltas:

   Long Call ≈ 0.55 to 0.45, one expiration later

   Short Call ≤ −0.25

Goals: Strong price rally that moves long calls ITM for profit; OTM short calls used to reduce entry cost.

Manage: If possible, roll short calls once. Otherwise, close the trade or let it expire worthless.

Profit: Close when profit is at or more than 30 percent.

Loss: Close for an 8 percent loss.

Calendar Bull Put

Strategy: Sell n Puts, ≤ 56 DTE

Buy n Puts, Lower Strike, 1 Expiration Later

Example:

Strategy	Buy/ Sell	Qty	Symbol	Trade Date	Exp. Date	Strike	Type	Price
Calendar	SELL	−5	AAOI	8/23/17	9/08/17	$60.00	PUT	$2.03
Bull Put	BUY	+5	AAOI	8/23/17	9/15/17	$55.00	PUT	−$1.38

Bias: Bullish * Risk: Low * Reward: Low

Calendar Bull Put Risk Profile

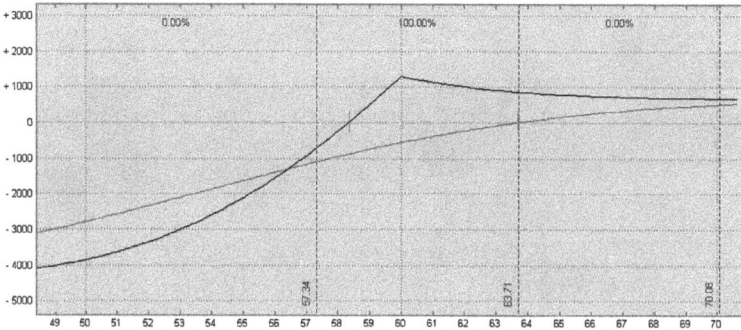

Price Chart: Uptrending

Current IV%: ≥ 60%

IV Rank: ≥ 70

Trade: Sell *n put* options; buy *n put* options, later expiration, lower strike.

Typical Strike Deltas:

   Short Put ≤ 0.30

   Long Put ≈ 2 to 4 strikes lower; based upon strike widths and premium

Goals: Collect premium; a rally in underlying moves both long and short puts farther OTM.

Manage: If possible, roll short puts once. Otherwise, close the trade as it approaches expiration for profit or let it expire worthless.

Profit: Close when profit is at or more than 30 percent.

Loss: Close for an 8 percent loss.

Diagonal Bull Call

Strategy: Sell *n* Calls, ≤ 56 DTE
Buy *n* Calls, Lower Strike, ≥ 90 DTE

Example:

Strategy	Buy/ Sell	Qty	Symbol	Trade Date	Exp. Date	Strike	Type	Price
Diagonal Bull Call	SELL	−5	FB	7/20/17	08/04/17	$172.50	CALL	$1.46
	BUY	+5	FB	7/20/17	10/20/17	$165.00	CALL	−$7.85

Bias: Bullish * Risk: Low * Reward: Moderate

Diagonal Bull Call Risk Profile

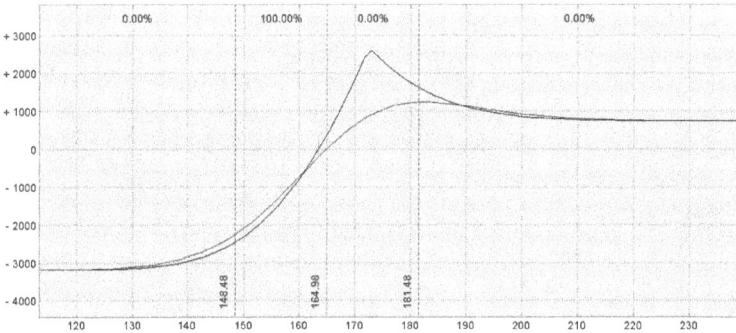

Price Chart: Uptrending

Current IV% ≤ 20%

IV Rank: ≤ 30

Trade: Buy *n* ATM or slightly OTM long-term calls; sell *n* calls several strikes above.

Typical Strike Deltas:

  Long Call ≈ 0.55 to 0.45

  Short Call ≤ −0.25 (higher strike, shorter expiration)

Goals: Rally moves long calls ITM for profit; short calls are rolled two or more times for additional premium.

Manage: If short calls remain OTM, collect more premium by rolling out to the next expiration and, if necessary, up to a higher strike.

Repeat until long calls move ITM and sell for profit. If underlying drops, close the trade.

Profit: Close when premium is greater than or equal to 30 percent (price near peak of plotline).

Loss: Close when premium is lesser than or equal to 8 percent (in case of a price drop).

Diagonal Bull Put

Strategy: Sell n Puts, Expire $\leq$ 56 DTE

Buy n Puts @ Lower Strike, Expire $\geq$ 90 DTE

Example:

Strategy	Buy/ Sell	Qty	Symbol	Trade Date	Exp. Date	Strike	Type	Price
Diagonal	SELL	−5	FB	7/20/17	08/11/17	$162.50	PUT	$4.58
Bull Put	BUY	+5	FB	7/20/17	10/20/17	$150.00	PUT	−$3.08

Bias: Bullish to Neutral * Risk: High to Moderate *
Reward: Moderate

Diagonal Bull Put Risk Profile

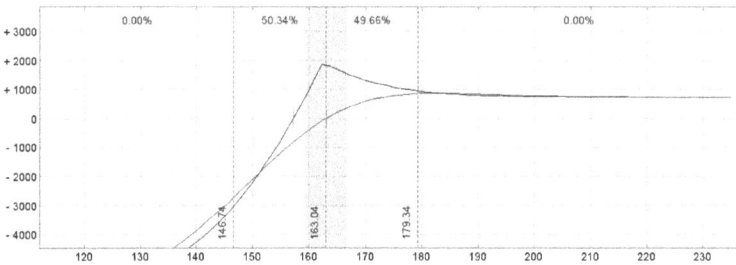

Price Chart: Uptrending

Current IV%: $\geq$ 60%

IV Rank: $\geq$ 70

Trade: Sell *n put* options; buy *n* put options, lower strike and several expirations later.

Typical Strike Deltas:

Short Put $\geq$ 0.25 or less

Long Put $\approx$ 2 or more strikes below short put for premium collection

Goals: Rally moves both long and short puts farther OTM; short puts are rolled two or more times for additional premium.

Manage: If short put remains OTM, roll to collect additional premium. If underlying drops, prevent short put from either expiring ITM or being exercised. Retain long put if profitable or sell long put to recover remaining premium.

Profit: Close when profit exceeds 30 percent.

Loss: Close when premium value loses 8 percent.

Calendar Straddle

Strategy: Sell n ATM Calls, $\leq$ 56 DTE

Buy n ATM Calls, Expire $\geq$ 90 DTE;

Sell n ATM Puts, Expire $\leq$ 56 DTE

Buy n ATM Puts, Expire $\geq$ 90 DTE

Example:

Strategy	Buy/ Sell	Qty	Symbol	Trade Date	Exp. Date	Strike	Type	Price
Calendar Straddle	SELL	−5	HA	07/5/17	07/21/17	$46.00	CALL	$1.38
	BUY	+5	HA	07/5/17	10/20/17	$47.00	CALL	−$3.80
	SELL	−5	HA	07/5/17	07/21/17	$46.00	PUT	$0.65
	BUY	+5	HA	07/5/17	10/20/17	$47.00	PUT	−$3.75

Bias: Neutral * Risk: High * Reward: Low

Calendar Straddle Risk Profile

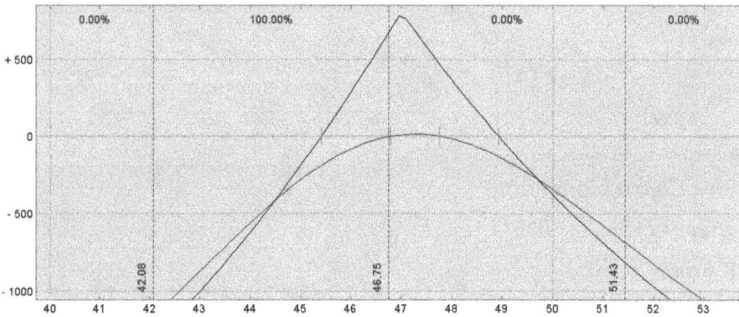

Price Chart: Uptrending (Example shows short options one strike below long options.)

Current IV%: $\geq$ 60%

IV Rank: $\geq$ 70

Trade: Sell n ATM put and call options that expire $\leq$ 56 DTE (20 to 30 DTE is typical); buy n ATM put and call options that expire $\geq$ 90 DTE.

Typical Strike Deltas:

ATM Long Call $\approx$ 0.50 Delta

ATM Long Put $\approx$ −0.50 Delta

ATM Short Call ≈ −0.50 Delta

ATM Short Put ≈ 0.50 Delta

Goals: This trade relies on Theta to reduce the premium values of the shorter-term short call and short put options faster than the loss in premium value of the longer-term long call and long put options. A strong move in either direction will benefit one of the long and short options, while the two losing options are closed to limit their loss in premium values.

Manage: When a price rally or drop occurs, close the losing long and short options. Keep the profitable long option as it moves deeper ITM and the profitable short option as it moves farther OTM.

Profit: Close when total original premium achieves 30 to 60 percent.

Loss: Close if an unexpected price reversal occurs and the remaining long and short option premium is lesser than or equal to 8 percent.

Neutral Calendar Call Straddle

Strategy: Sell *n* ATM Calls, ≤ 56 DTE
Buy *n* ATM Calls, ≥ 90 DTE

Example:

Strategy	Buy/ Sell	Qty	Symbol	Trade Date	Exp. Date	Strike	Type	Price
Neutral Calendar Call Straddle	SELL	−5	HA	07/5/17	07/21/17	$47.00	CALL	$0.88
	BUY	+5	HA	07/5/17	10/20/17	$47.00	CALL	−$3.80

Bias: Bullish to Neutral * Risk: High * Reward: Low

Neutral Calendar Call Straddle Risk Profile

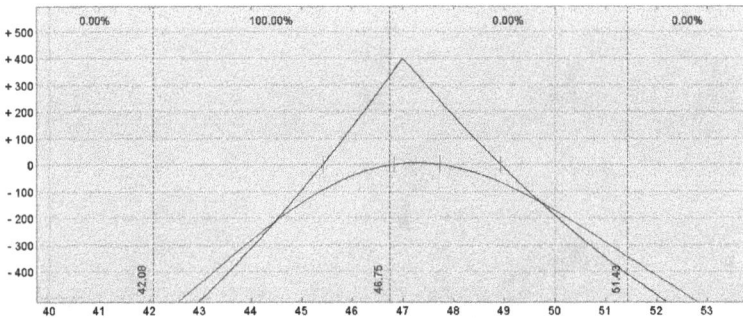

Price Chart: Neutral to slight upward price trend

Current IV%: ≈ 50%

IV Rank: ≈ 40 to 60

Trade: Buy *n* ATM call options, ≥ 90 DTE; sell *n* ATM call options, ≤ 56 DTE.

Typical Strike Deltas:

  Long Call ≈ 0.48 to 0.52

  Short Call ≈ −0.48 to −0.52

Goals: This trade relies on a price rally in the underlying security which moves the long call deeper ITM for an increase in premium. The premium received from the short call offsets a portion of the premium paid for the long call.

Manage: If a price rally occurs according to the trader's bullish bias, the short call is closed and the long call moves deeper ITM. When the long call's premium is sufficiently high, the long call is sold for profit. If retained, farther OTM short calls can be sold for additional premium in the same way the diagonal bull call strategy is managed. If converted to a diagonal bull call, roll the short call out and up to collect additional premium.

Profit: Close when total premium is greater than or equal to 30 percent.

Loss: Close when total premium is lesser than or equal to 8 percent (in case of a price drop).

Iron Condor

Strategy: Sell n OTM Calls, Expire ≤ 56 DTE
Buy n OTM Calls, Higher Strike, Same Expiry
Sell n OTM Puts, Same Expiry
Buy n OTM Puts, Lower Strike, Same Expiry

Example:

Strategy	Buy/ Sell	Qty	Symbol	Trade Date	Exp. Date	Strike	Type	Price
Iron Condor	SELL	−5	AAPL	08/03/17	08/25/17	$162.50	CALL	$0.63
	BUY	+5	AAPL	08/03/17	08/25/17	$167.50	CALL	−$0.20
	SELL	−5	AAPL	08/03/17	08/25/17	$150.00	PUT	$1.00
	BUY	+5	AAPL	08/03/17	08/25/17	$147.00	PUT	−$0.54

Bias: Neutral * Risk: Low * Reward: Low

Iron Condor Risk Profile

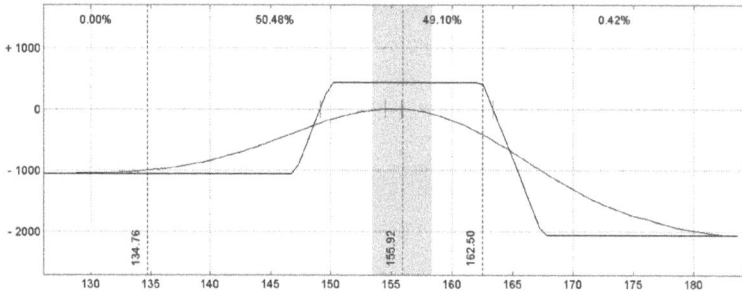

Price Chart: Neutral to slight downward price trend

Current IV%: ≈ 50%

IV Rank: ≈ 40 to 60

Trade: Sell *n* OTM call options; buy *n* OTM call options, higher strike; sell *n* OTM put options; buy *n* OTM put options, lower strike (all options at same expiration, ≤ 56 DTE).

Typical Strike Deltas:

   Short Call ≤ −0.25

   Long Call ≈ 2 or more strikes farther OTM than short call

   Short Put ≤ 0.25

   Long Put ≈ 2 or more strikes farther OTM than short put

Goals: The goal is to retain the premium collected when opened and for the vertical bull put and vertical bear call spreads to remain OTM through option expirations or until closed for a profit.

Manage: If the price of the underlying security remains within a narrow range, let the options expire worthless. If a price rally or drop occurs and threatens one of the vertical spreads, close the vulnerable position and retain the safe spread until it either expires worthless or can be closed for a reasonable profit.

Profit: Close when this strategy achieves a profit of 30 percent or more.

Loss: Close when a loss in premium value becomes 8 percent or less.

Jade Lizard

Strategy: Sell *n* OTM Calls, ≤ 56 DTE
Buy *n* OTM Calls, Higher Strike, Same Expiry
Sell *n* OTM Puts, Same Expiry

Example:

Strategy	Buy/ Sell	Qty	Symbol	Trade Date	Exp. Date	Strike	Type	Price
Jade Lizard	SELL	−10	BIDU	07/20/17	08/18/17	$210.00	CALL	$1.22
	BUY	+10	BIDU	07/20/17	08/18/17	$220.00	CALL	−$0.49
	SELL	−10	BIDU	07/20/17	08/18/17	$175.00	PUT	$1.24

Bias: Neutral * Risk: High * Reward: Low

Jade Lizard Risk Profile

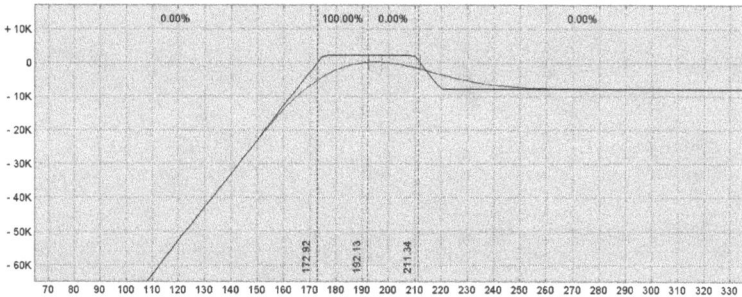

Price Chart: Neutral; may be experiencing a small upward trend.

Current IV%: ≈ 50%

IV Rank: ≈ 40 to 60

Trade: Sell *n* OTM call options; buy *n* OTM call options, higher strike; sell *n* OTM put options (all options at same expiration, ≤ 56 DTE).

Typical Strike Deltas:

   Short Call ≤ −0.25

   Long Call ≈ 2 strikes farther OTM than the short call

   Short Put ≤ 0.25

Goals: This trade retains the premium collected when opened as long as both the short put and vertical bear call spread remain OTM.

Manage: If the price of the underlying security remains within a narrow range, let the options expire worthless. If a price rally or drop occurs that threatens the short put or the bear call vertical spread, close the vulnerable position and retain the safe position until it either expires worthless or can be closed for a profit.

Profit: Close when this strategy achieves a profit of 30 percent or more. If the options remain OTM, consider letting the trade expire worthless.

Loss: Close when a loss in premium value becomes 8 percent or less.

Twisted Sister

Strategy: Sell n OTM Puts, $\leq$ 56 DTE

Buy n OTM Puts, Lower Strike, Same Expiry

Sell n OTM Calls, Same Expiry

Example:

Strategy	Buy/ Sell	Qty	Symbol	Trade Date	Exp. Date	Strike	Type	Price
Twisted Sister	SELL	−10	DAL	07/13/17	07/21/17	$57.00	CALL	−$0.73
	BUY	+10	DAL	07/13/17	07/21/17	$52.50	PUT	−$0.36
	SELL	−10	DAL	07/13/17	07/21/17	$51.50	PUT	$0.26

Bias: Neutral to Bearish * Risk: High * Reward: Low

Twisted Sister Risk Profile

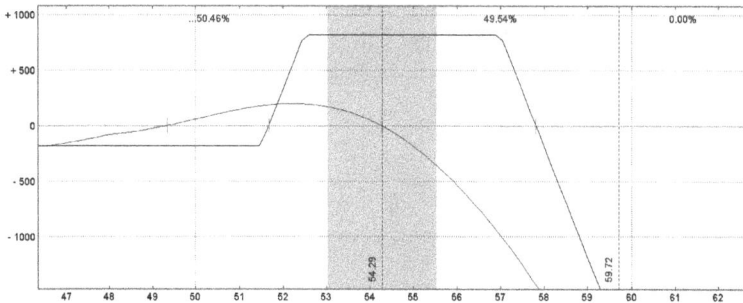

Price Chart: Neutral; may be experiencing small downward trend.

Current IV%: $\approx$ 50%

IV Rank: $\approx$ 40 to 60

Trade: Sell n OTM call options; sell n OTM put options; buy n OTM put options, lower strike. (All options expire $\leq$ 56 DTE; $\approx$ 30 days DTE is typical.)

Typical Strike Deltas:

  Short Put $\leq$ 0.25

  Long Put $\approx$ 2 or more strikes farther OTM than short put

  Short Call $\leq$ −0.20 (or even less when premium is adequate)

Goals: This trade retains the premium collected when opened as long as both the short call and vertical bull put spread remain OTM.

Manage: If the price of the underlying security remains within a narrow range, let the options expire worthless. If a price rally or drop occurs that threatens the short call or the vertical bull put spread, close the vulnerable position and retain the safe position until it either expires worthless or can be closed for a reasonable profit. This trade includes uncovered short calls requiring the trader to have the highest option trading level.

Profit: Close when this strategy achieves a profit of 30 percent or more.

Loss: Close when a loss in premium value becomes 8 percent or less.

Reverse Iron Condor

Strategy: Buy n OTM Calls, ≤ 56 DTE
Sell n OTM Calls, Higher Strike, Same Expiry
Buy n OTM Puts, Same Expiry
Sell n OTM Puts, Lower Strike, Same Expiry

Example:

Strategy	Buy/ Sell	Qty	Symbol	Trade Date	Exp. Date	Strike	Type	Price
Reverse Iron Condor	BUY	+5	AAPL	11/10/17	12/01/17	$180.00	CALL	−$1.03
	SELL	−5	AAPL	11/10/17	12/01/17	$185.00	CALL	$0.33
	BUY	+5	AAPL	11/10/17	12/01/17	$170.00	PUT	−$1.23
	SELL	−5	AAPL	11/10/17	12/01/17	$165.00	PUT	$0.51

Bias: Neutral * Risk: Low * Reward: Low

Reverse Iron Condor Risk Profile

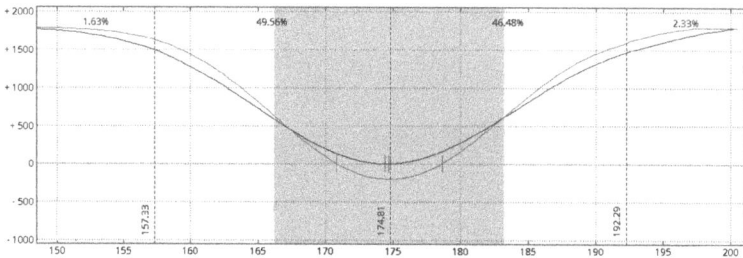

Price Chart: Neutral; may be experiencing small upward trend.

Current IV%: ≈ 50%

IV Rank: ≈ 35 to 65

Trade: Buy n OTM call options; sell n OTM call options, higher strike; buy n OTM put options; sell n OTM put options, lower strike. (All options expire ≤ 56 DTE.)

Typical Strike Deltas:

Short Put ≤ 0.25

Long Put ≈ 2 strikes farther OTM than the short put

Long Call ≤ 0.20 (or less when premium is adequate)

Short Call ≈ 2 strikes farther OTM than the long call

Goals: This trade, which combines a bear put and a bear call, requires a strong directional price move, either up or down, to return a profit.

Manage: When a large directional price breakout occurs, the losing long and short options are closed. The remaining long option will move deeper ITM while the remaining short option will move farther OTM, both for profit.

Profit: Close when this strategy achieves a profit of 30 percent or more.

Loss: Close when an 8 percent loss in premium value occurs.

Condor

Strategy: Buy n ITM Calls, ≤ 56 DTE
Sell n ITM Calls, Higher Strike, Same Expiry
Sell n OTM Calls, Same Expiry
Buy n OTM Calls, Higher Strike, Same Expiry

Example:

Strategy	Buy/ Sell	Qty	Symbol	Trade Date	Exp. Date	Strike	Type	Price
`Condor	BUY	+5	OLED	09/06/17	10/20/17	$125.00	CALL	−$12.00
	SELL	−5	OLED	09/06/17	10/20/17	$130.00	CALL	$8.75
	SELL	−5	OLED	09/06/17	10/20/17	$135.00	CALL	$6.30
	BUY	+5	OLED	09/06/17	10/20/17	$140.00	CALL	−$4.35

Bias: Bullish * Risk: Low * Reward: Low

Condor Risk Profile

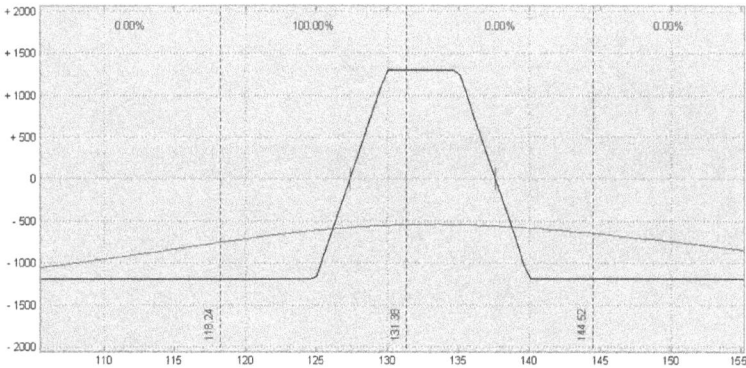

Price Chart: Neutral; may be experiencing small upward price movement.

Current IV%: ≈ 50%

IV Rank: ≈ 35 to 65

Trade: Buy *n* ITM call options; sell *n* ITM call options, higher strike; sell *n* OTM call options; buy *n* OTM call options, higher strike. (All options expire ≤ 56 DTE.)

Strike Deltas:

Long ITM Call ≥ 0.55

Short ITM Call ≥ −0.50, higher strike

Short OTM Call ≤ −0.50

Long OTM Call ≤ 0.50, higher strike

Goals: An examination of the strikes of this trade and its risk profile shows how a small increase in the value of the underlying increases the net premium values of this strategy.

Manage: If the price of the underlying security increases by a few dollars, this trade can be closed for a few hundred dollars more than the premium originally paid to open it. If a month to several weeks remain and the ITM long call moves deeper ITM, the trader can retain the long call and sell an OTM call option for additional premium collection. However, Theta will increase its daily reduction of the long call's premium value. This requires a careful examination of the premium received from a round of short OTM calls compared with the daily premium being lost by the remaining long ITM call.

Profit: Close when this strategy achieves a profit of 10 percent or more.

Loss: Close immediately if the price of the underlying begins to trend downward.

Short Condor

Strategy: Sell *n* ITM Calls, ≤ 56 DTE

Buy *n* ITM Calls, Higher Strike, Same Expiry

Buy *n* OTM Calls, Same Expiry

Sell *n* OTM Calls, Higher Strike, Same Expiry

Example:

Strategy	Buy/ Sell	Qty	Symbol	Trade Date	Exp. Date	Strike	Type	Price
Short Condor	SELL	−5	QQQ	09/06/17	10/20/17	$140.00	CALL	$6.20
	BUY	+5	QQQ	09/06/17	10/20/17	$144.00	CALL	−$3.31
	BUY	+5	QQQ	09/06/17	10/20/17	$145.00	CALL	−$2.68
	SELL	−5	QQQ	09/06/17	10/20/17	$149.00	CALL	$0.86

Bias: Bearish * Risk: Low * Reward: Low

Short Condor Risk Profile

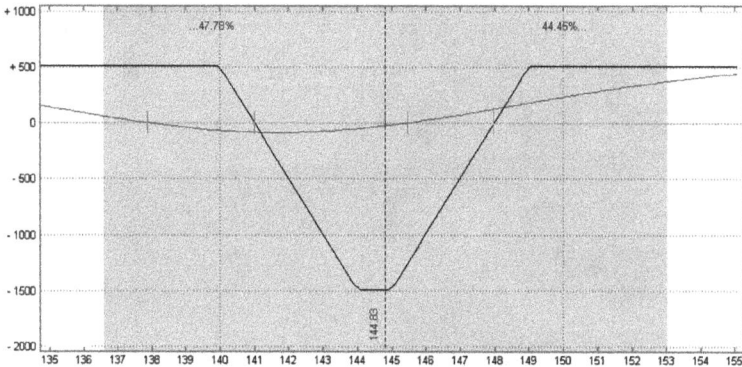

Price Chart: A series of strong directional price moves

Current IV%: ≤ 25% (to reduce premium values)

IV Rank: ≈ 10 to 20

Trade: Sell *n* ITM call options; buy *n* ITM call options, higher strike; buy *n* OTM call options; sell *n* OTM call options, higher strike. (All options expire ≤ 56 DTE.)

Strike Deltas:

Short ITM Call ≥ −0.50

Long ITM Call ≥ 0.50, higher strike

Long OTM Call ≤ 0.50

Short OTM Call ≤ −0.50, higher strike

Goals: An examination of the strikes of this trade and its risk profile shows how a large increase or decrease in the value of the underlying is required for this trade to offset the cost of entry. Therefore, a strong price move and careful trade management is essential for this strategy to return a profit.

Manage: Watch for a strong directional price move. Respond by closing the losing options and retaining the profitable options. For example, if the price of the underlying drops, retain the short calls and sell the long calls. Respond to a rally by closing the short calls and retaining the long calls. Consider using the long calls to anchor a bull put spread or to create a long call butterfly in response to an upward price move.

Profit: Close when the retained options achieve a profit of 30 percent or more.

Loss: Close if this trade becomes unmanageable for a return in profit.

Short Strangle

Strategy: Sell *n* OTM Calls, ≤ 56 DTE
Sell *n* OTM Puts, Same Expiry

Example:

Strategy	Buy/ Sell	Qty	Symbol	Trade Date	Exp. Date	Strike	Type	Price
Short	SELL	−5	AAOI	08/08/17	08/18/17	$85.00	CALL	$1.78
Strangle	SELL	−5	AAOI-	08/08/17	08/18/17	$60.00	PUT	$2.08

Bias: Neutral * Risk: High * Reward: Low

Short Strangle Risk Profile

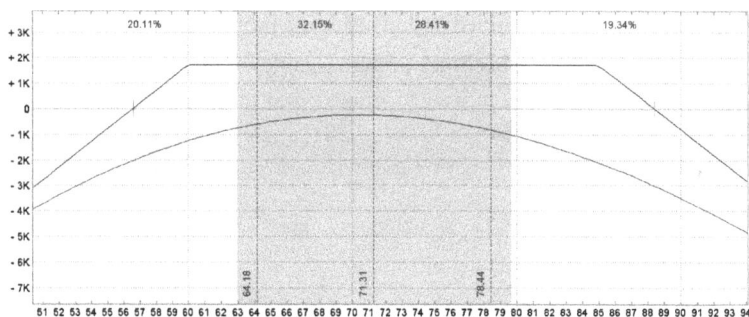

Price Chart: Moving sideways (neutral)

Current IV%: ≥ 40% (to increase premium values)

IV Rank: ≥ 50

Trade: Sell *n* OTM put options; sell *n* OTM call options. (All options expire ≤ 56 DTE.)

Typical Strike Deltas:
   Short OTM Calls ≤ −0.25
   Short OTM Puts ≤ 0.25

Goals: Premium collection from short options placed at far OTM strikes that are unlikely to become ITM prior to expiration.

Manage: Monitor this trade to ensure that the strikes of the short put and short call options remain safely OTM. If one of the options is threatened, either close it or buy a long option 1 or 2 strikes farther OTM for insurance. If the options remain OTM, consider letting them expire worthless to achieve this strategy's maximum profit. This trade includes uncovered short calls requiring the trader to have the highest option trading level.

Profit: Close when the remaining options achieve a profit of 30 percent or let these short options expire worthless for 100 percent profit.

Loss: Close one of the short options if it approaches the ATM strike. This can result in a net premium loss that exceeds 30 percent.

Long Strangle

Strategy: Buy n OTM Calls, Expire ≥ 90 DTE
Buy n OTM Puts, Same Expiry

Example:

Strategy	Buy/ Sell	Qty	Symbol	Trade Date	Exp. Date	Strike	Type	Price
Long	BUY	+5	QQQ	08/08/17	12/15/17	$143.00	CALL	−$5.89
Strangle	BUY	+5	QQQ	08/08/17	12/15/17	$145.00	PUT	−$4.67

Bias: Strongly Bullish or Strongly Bearish * Risk: Low * Reward: High

Long Strangle Risk Profile

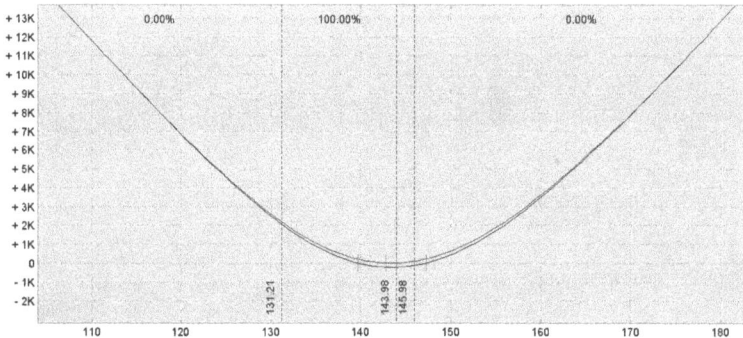

Price Chart: A series of strong directional price moves

Current IV%: ≤ 25% (to reduce premium values)

IV Rank: ≈ 10 to 20

Trade: Buy *n* slightly OTM call options; buy *n* slightly OTM put options. (All options expire ≥ 90 DTE.)

Strike Deltas: (both 1 to 3 strikes OTM)

   Long OTM Call ≥ 0.50

   Long OTM Put ≤ −0.50

Goals: A strong directional price move benefits one of the long options as it moves deeper ITM. The opposite long option is closed as soon as the trader is confident in a sustained directional price move.

Manage: Watch for a strong directional price move. Respond by closing the losing long options and retaining the profitable long options as they move deeper ITM. Once a satisfactory profit is achieved, sell the remaining long options before a price reversal occurs.

Profit: Close when the remaining long options achieve a profit of 30 percent or more.

Loss: Close if the directional move changes and begins to reduce the value of the remaining option premium.

Covered Short Strangle

Strategy: Buy or Own n × 100 Shares,

Sell n OTM Calls, Expire ≤ 56 DTE

Sell n OTM Puts, Same Expiry

Example:

Strategy	Buy/Sell	Qty	Symbol	Trade Date	Exp. Date	Strike	Type	Price
Covered	BUY/OWN	1,000	AOII				STOCK	−$68.70
Short	SELL	−10	AOII	08/09/17	09/15/17	$80.00	CALL	$1.88
Strangle	SELL	−10	AOII	08/09/17	09/15/17	$55.00	PUT	$1.30

Bias: Bullish to Neutral Bearish * Risk: Moderate to Low *
Reward: Moderate to Low

Covered Short Strangle Risk Profile

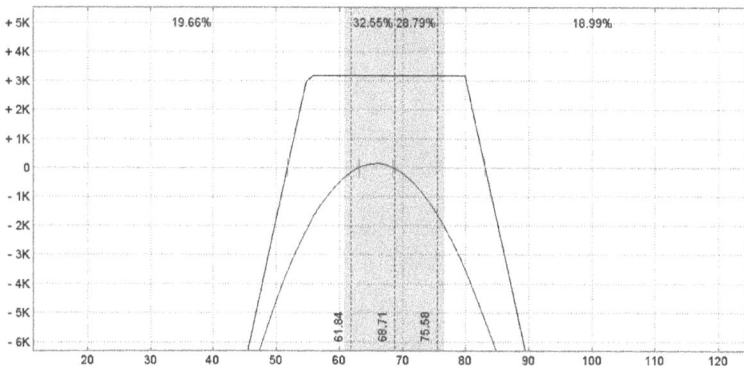

Price Chart: Moving sideways (neutral) to slightly upward

Current IV%: ≥ 40% (to increase premium values)

IV Rank: ≥ 50

Trade: Sell n OTM put options; sell n OTM call options. (All options expire ≤ 56 DTE.)

Typical Strike Deltas:

Short OTM Calls ≤ −0.25

Short OTM Puts ≤ 0.25

Goals: Premium collection from short options placed 1 standard deviation or more OTM at strikes that are unlikely to become ITM prior to expiration.

Manage: Monitor this trade to ensure that the strikes of the short put and short call options remain safely OTM. If a price rally moves close to the short call, the covering stock will benefit from the price increase. This may encourage the trader to sell the stock and buy to close the short puts and short calls. The short puts may also be held until they expire worthless. If the short call options remain OTM, consider trading another covered short strangle or a covered call. If the stock price drops, the short put should be closed to prevent it from being exercised and the short call options should be retained, rolled for profit, or, as mentioned, permitted to expire worthless.

Profit: Close when the short options achieve a profit of 50 percent or more or let these short options expire worthless for 100 percent profit. If the price of the underlying rallies, consider collecting additional profit by selling the stock.

Loss: Close one of the short options if it approaches the ATM strike. This can result in a net loss in premium exceeding 30 percent.

Long Guts Strangle

Strategy: Buy n ATM Calls, ≥ 90 DTE
Buy n ATM Puts, ≥ 90 DTE

Example:

Strategy	Buy/ Sell	Qty	Symbol	Trade Date	Exp. Date	Strike	Type	Price
Long Guts	BUY	+5	DAL	08/09/17	12/15/17	$52.50	CALL	−$1.74
Strangle	BUY	+5	DAL	08/09/17	12/12/17	$48.00	PUT	−$2.47

Bias: Strongly Bullish or Strongly Bearish * Risk: Low *
Reward: High

Long Guts Strangle Risk Profile

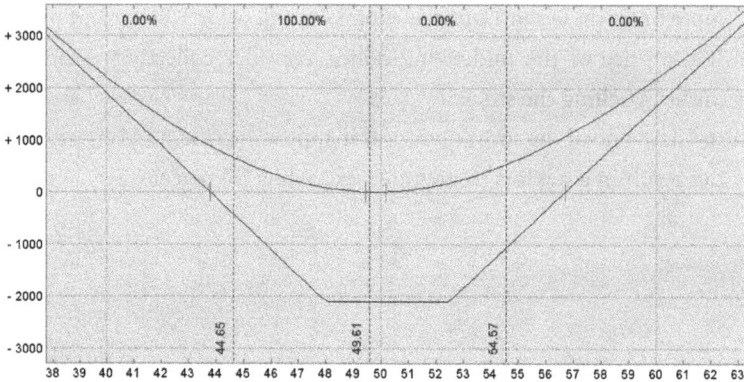

Price Chart: A series of strong directional price moves

Current IV%: ≤ 25% (to reduce premium values)

IV Rank: ≈ 10 to 20

Trade: Buy *n* ATM call options; buy *n* ATM put options. (All options expire ≥ 90 DTE.)

Strike Deltas: (both 1 to 3 strikes OTM)

  Long OTM Call ≥ 0.50

  Long OTM Put ≤ −0.50

Goals: A strong directional price move benefits one of the long options as it moves deeper ITM. The opposite long option is closed as soon as the trader is confident that the directional price move will continue.

Manage: Watch for a strong directional price move. Respond by selling the losing long option when it begins to move OTM. Retain the profitable long options as they move deeper ITM for profit. Once a satisfactory profit is achieved, sell the remaining long options.

Profit: Close when the remaining options achieve a profit of 30 percent or more.

Loss: Close if the directional move changes and begins to reduce the value of the remaining long options.

Short Straddle

Strategy: Sell *n* ATM Calls, ≤ 56 DTE
Sell *n* ATM Puts, Same Expiry

Example:

Strategy	Buy/ Sell	Qty	Symbol	Trade Date	Exp. Date	Strike	Type	Price
Short	SELL	−10	EXAS	07/25/17	08/18/17	$38.00	CALL	$0.90
Straddle	SELL	−10	EXAS	07/25/17	08/18/17	$38.00	PUT	$1.83

Bias: Neutral * Risk: High * Reward: Low

Short Straddle Risk Profile

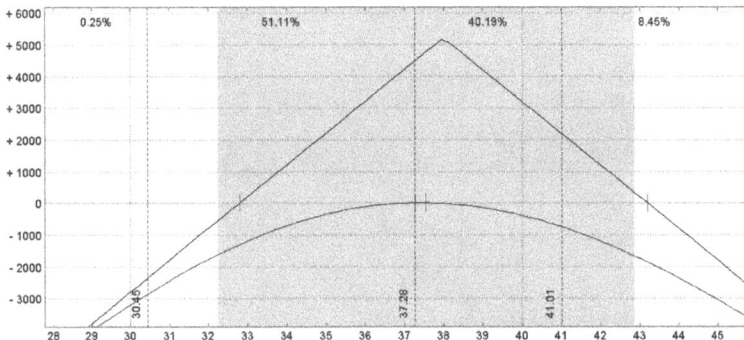

Price Chart: Strong directional price moves

Current IV%: ≥ 40% (to increase premium values)

IV Rank: ≈ 50

Trade: Sell *n* ATM call options; sell *n* ATM put options. (All options expire ≤ 56 DTE; 30 DTE is typical.)

Strike Deltas: (both ATM)

   Short ATM Call ≈ −0.50

   Short ATM Put ≈ 0.50

Goals: A strong, sustained directional price move signals the trader to buy to close the losing short options that begin to move ITM and retain the short options that begin to move OTM. As evident in the above-mentioned risk profile, holding both the put and call options causes this trade to begin losing premium value from a price move in either direction.

Manage: Watch for a strong directional price move. Buy to close the losing short option as it begins to move ITM and becomes more expensive to close. Retain the profitable short options as they move farther OTM for profit. Once a satisfactory profit is achieved, either buy the remaining short options or let them expire worthless. This trade includes uncovered short calls requiring the trader to have the highest option trading level.

Profit: Close when the remaining options achieves a profit of 30 percent or more.

Loss: Close if the price move reverses direction and begins to increase the value of the remaining short options.

Long Straddle

Strategy: Buy *n* ATM Calls, ≥ 90 DTE
Buy *n* ATM Puts, Same Expiry

Example:

Strategy	Buy/ Sell	Qty	Symbol	Trade Date	Exp. Date	Strike	Type	Price
Long	BUY	1	BIDU	08/10/17	12/15/17	$230.00	CALL	−$16.55
Straddle	BUY	1	BIDU	08/10/17	12/15/17	$230.00	PUT	−$15.03

Bias: Bullish or Bearish * Risk: Low * Reward: High

Long Straddle Risk Profile

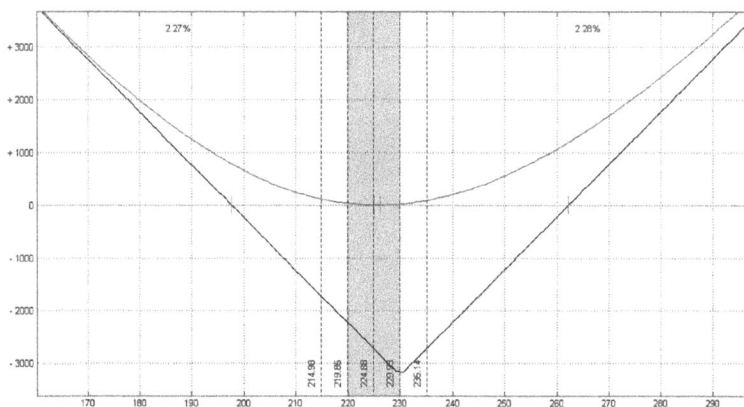

Price Chart: A series of strong directional price moves

Current IV%: ≤ 25% (to reduce premium values)

IV Rank: ≈ 10 to 20

Trade: Buy *n* ATM call options; buy *n* ATM put options. (All options expire ≥ 90 DTE.)

Strike Deltas: (both strikes ATM)

   Long ATM Call ≈ 0.50

   Long ATM Put ≈ −0.50

Goals: A strong directional price move benefits one of the ATM long options as it moves deeper ITM. The opposite long option is sold as soon as the trader is confident in a sustained directional price move.

Manage: Watch for a strong directional price move. Respond by selling the losing long options for as much premium as possible and retaining the profitable long options as they move deeper ITM. Once a satisfactory profit is achieved, sell the remaining long options. If ample time remains, consider using the long options to cover a bull call or a bear put to collect additional premium.

Profit: Close when the remaining option achieves a profit of 30 percent or more.

Loss: Close if the directional move changes and begins to reduce the value of the remaining options.

Strap

Strategy: Buy 2n ATM Calls, Expire ≥ 90 DTE
Buy n ATM Puts, Same Expiry

Example:

Strategy	Buy/ Sell	Qty	Symbol	Trade Date	Exp. Date	Strike	Type	Price
Strap	BUY	+10	BAC	07/11/17	10/20/17	$37.00	CALL	−$1.07
	BUY	+5	BAC	07/11/17	10/20/17	$37.00	PUT	−$1.47

Bias: Bullish * Risk: Low * Reward: High

Strap Risk Profile

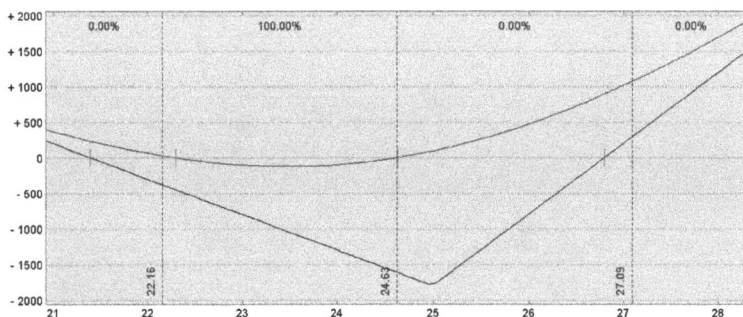

Price Chart: A series of strong directional price moves on an upward trending security

Current IV%: ≤ 25% (to reduce premium values)

IV Rank: ≈ 10 to 25

Trade: Buy 2n ATM call options; buy n ATM put options. (All options expire ≥ 90 DTE.)

Strike Deltas: (both strikes ATM)

   Long ATM Calls ≈ 0.50

   Long ATM Puts ≈ −0.50

Goals: A strong directional price move benefits one of the ATM long options as it moves deeper ITM. The strap option strategy favors a rally rather than a drop because of the 2:1 call-to-put ratio. The opposite long option is sold as soon as the trader is confident of a sustained directional price move.

Manage: Watch for a strong directional price move. Respond by selling the losing long options to recover as much premium as possible. Retain the profitable long options as they move deeper ITM. Once a satisfactory profit is achieved, sell the remaining long options. If ample time remains, consider using the long options to cover a bull call or a bear put vertical to collect additional premium.

Profit: Close when the remaining option achieves a profit of 30 percent or more.

Loss: Close if the directional move changes and begins to reduce the value of the remaining options.

Strip

Strategy: Buy 2n ATM Puts, Expire ≥ 90 DTE
Buy n ATM Calls, Same Expiry

Example:

Strategy	Buy/ Sell	Qty	Symbol	Trade Date	Exp. Date	Strike	Type	Price
Strip	BUY	+10	GE	07/11/17	10/20/17	$27.00	PUT	−$1.42
	BUY	+5	GE	07/11/17	10/20/17	$27.00	CALL	−$0.66

Bias: Bearish * Risk: Low * Reward: High

Strip Risk Profile

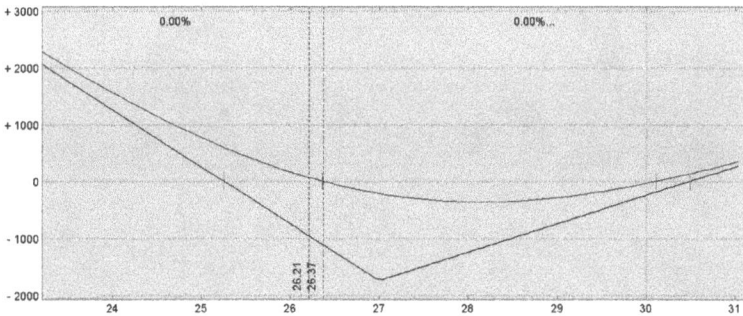

Price Chart: A series of strong directional price moves on a downward trending security

Current IV%: ≤ 25% (to reduce premium values)

IV Rank: ≈ 10 to 25

Trade: Buy 2n ATM put options; buy n ATM call options (All options expire ≥ 90 DTE.)

Strike Deltas: (both strikes ATM)

　　Long ATM Calls ≈ 0.50

　　Long ATM Puts ≈ −0.50

Goals: A strong directional price move benefits one of the ATM long options as it moves deeper ITM. The strip option strategy favors a price drop rather than a price rally. The opposite long option is sold as soon as the trader is confident that the directional price move will continue. The strip option strategy favors a drop rather than a rally because of the 2:1 put-to-call ratio.

Manage: Watch for a strong directional price move. Respond by selling the losing long options to recover as much premium as possible. Retain the long options as they move deeper ITM. Once a satisfactory profit is achieved, sell the remaining long options. If ample time remains, consider using the long options to cover a bull call or a bear put vertical in order to collect additional premium.

Profit: Close when the remaining options achieve a profit of 30 percent or more.

Loss: Close if the directional move changes and begins to reduce the value of the remaining options.

Call Ratio Spread

Strategy: Buy *n* ATM Calls, Expire ≤ 56 DTE
Sell 2*n* or 3*n* OTM Calls, Same Expiration

Example:

Strategy	Buy/ Sell	Qty	Symbol	Trade Date	Exp. Date	Strike	Type	Price
Call Ratio Spread	BUY	+1	FB	08/10/17	09/15/17	$175	CALL	−$3.54
	SELL	−3	FB	08/10/17	09/15/17	$180	CALL	$1.75

Bias: Bullish * Risk: High * Reward: Low

Call Ratio Spread Risk Profile

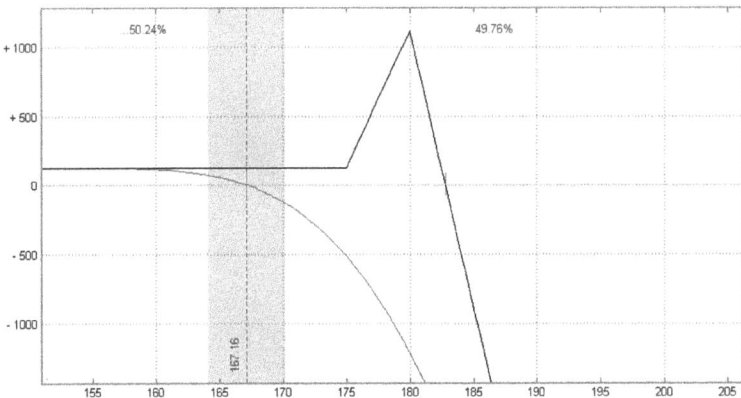

Price Chart: Uptrending off support

Current IV%: ≤ 20%

IV Rank: ≤ 30

Trade: Buy *n* ATM call options; sell 2*n* or 3*n* OTM call options at least 1 standard deviation farther OTM.

Typical Strike Deltas:

  Long Calls ≈ 0.50 to 0.45

  Short Calls ≈ −0.25

Goals: Retain the credit in premium received from selling the multiple short calls as profit when this strategy is entered. A strong rally in the price of the underlying moves the long calls deeper ITM for an increase in premium and makes this trade even more profitable.

Manage: If the long call moves deeper ITM from a rally in the price of the underlying security, or even if a price drop occurs, the premium collected when this trade was entered is retained as profit. If the price of the underlying rallies to the strike of the multiple short calls, close the trade for the profit as the price approaches the peak of the risk profile's plotline. If the price rally exceeds the strike of the short call options, close the trade before it begins to lose premium. **Do not let the short calls expire ITM.** This trade includes uncovered short calls requiring the trader to have the highest option trading level.

Profit: Close when this trade returns a profit that is greater than or equal to 30 percent.

Loss: Close this trade when the underlying is close to the strike of the OTM short calls.

Put Ratio Spread

Strategy: Buy n ATM Puts, ≤ 56 DTE
Sell 2n or 3n OTM Puts, Same Expiration

Example:

Strategy	Buy/ Sell	Qty	Symbol	Trade Date	Exp. Date	Strike	Type	Price
Put Ratio Spread	BUY	+3	AAOI	08/11/17	09/15/17	$65.00	PUT	−$5.10
	SELL	−6	AAOI	08/11/17	09/15/17	$60.00	PUT	$2.88

Bias: Bullish * Risk: High * Reward: Low

Put Ratio Spread Risk Profile

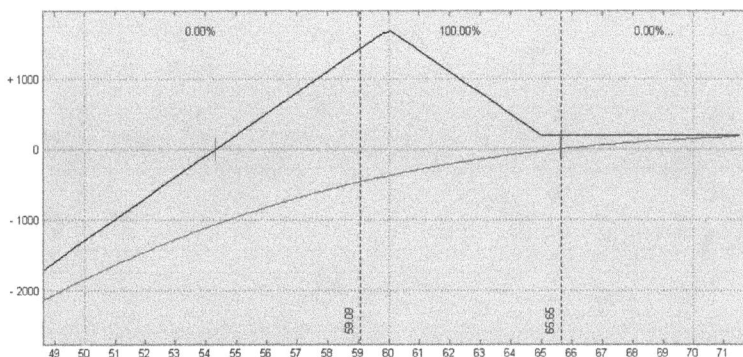

Price Chart: Downtrending off of resistance

Current IV%: ≤ 20%

IV Rank: ≤ 30

Trade: Buy n ATM put options; sell 2n or 3n OTM put options at least 1 standard deviation farther OTM depending on the strike width increments and premium values.

Typical Strike Deltas:

Long Puts ≈ −0.50 to −0.45

Short Puts ≈ 0.25 (3 to 5 strikes farther OTM depending on the strike width increments and premium values)

Goals: Keep the credit in premium received from selling the multiple short puts when this strategy is entered. A strong drop in the price of the underlying moves the long puts deeper ITM for an increase in premium and makes this trade even more profitable.

Manage: If the long put moves deeper ITM from a drop in the price of the underlying security, or even if a price rally occurs, the premium collected when this trade is entered is retained. If the price of the underlying drops to the strike of the multiple short puts, close the trade for the profit as the price approaches the peak of the risk profile's plotline. If a price drop exceeds the strike of the short put options, close the trade before it begins to lose. **Do not let the short puts expire ITM.** This trade includes uncovered short calls requiring the trader to have the highest option trading level.

Profit: Close when this trade returns a profit that is greater than or equal to 30 percent.

Loss: Close this trade when the underlying is close to the strike of the OTM short puts.

Diagonal Call Ratio Spread

Strategy: Sell 2n or 3n OTM Calls, ≤ 56 DTE

Buy n ATM Calls, Expire ≥ 90 DTE

Example:

Strategy	Buy/ Sell	Qty	Symbol	Trade Date	Exp. Date	Strike	Type	Price
Diagonal Call Ratio Spread	BUY	+5	WDC	08/11/17	01/19/18	$80.00	CALL	−$7.63
	SELL	−10	WDC	08/11/17	09/08//17	$85.00	CALL	$1.33

Bias: Bullish or Neutral * Risk: High * Reward: Low

Diagonal Call Ratio Spread Risk Profile

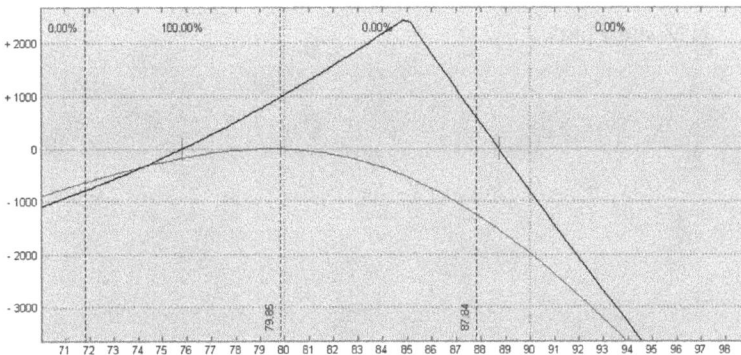

Price Chart: Uptrending off support

Current IV%: ≤ 20%

IV Rank: ≤ 30

Trade: Buy n ATM call options that expire ≥ DTE; sell 2n or 3n OTM call options higher strike that expire ≤ 56 DTE.

Typical Strike Deltas:

Long Calls ≈ 0.50 to 0.45

Short Calls ≤ −0.25

Goals: Use two or three short calls to reduce the premium required to enter this strategy or for premium collection. Close the trade for profit when the price rallies sufficiently to achieve profit or if it drops to approximately $80 and remains profitable.

Manage: If the long call moves deeper ITM from an expected rally in the price of the underlying security, close the trade for the profit as indicated in the risk profile. Alternatively, retain the long calls, which are now ITM, and either close or roll the short calls out and up for additional premium. If the price of the underlying drops, sell the long calls and keep the short calls that move farther OTM. Finally, buy to close the short calls for less premium than originally received or let them expire worthless. This trade includes uncovered short calls requiring the trader to have the highest option trading level.

Profit: Close when the underlying is close to the strike of the short calls.

Loss: Close the long calls if the price of the underlying begins to trend downward.

Diagonal Put Ratio Spread

Strategy: Sell 2n or 3n OTM Puts, ≤ 56 DTE

Buy n ATM Puts, Expire ≥ 90 DTE

Example:

Strategy	Buy/ Sell	Qty	Symbol	Trade Date	Exp. Date	Strike	Type	Price
Diagonal Put Ratio Spread	BUY	+2	VIX	08/12/17	11/15/17	$15.00	PUT	−$2.11
	SELL	−6	VIX	08/12/17	9/06/17	$13.00	PUT	$0.96

Bias: Bullish or Neutral * Risk: High * Reward: Low

Diagonal Put Ratio Spread Risk Profile

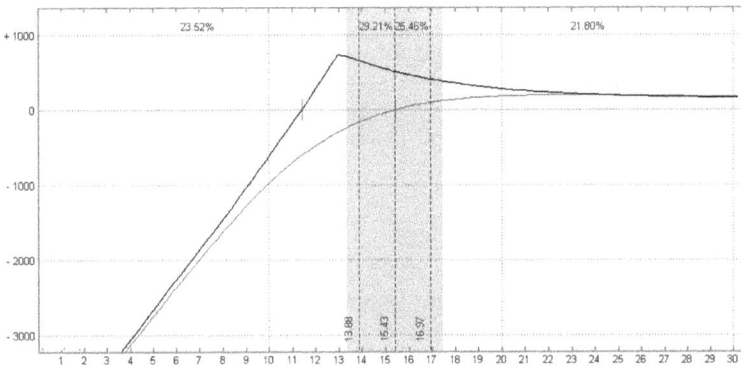

Price Chart: Downtrending off of resistance

Current IV%: ≤ 20%

IV Rank: ≤ 30

Trade: Buy n ATM put options; sell 2n or 3n OTM put options lower strike.

Typical Strike Deltas:

Long Puts ≈ −0.50 to −0.45

Short Puts ≈ ≤ 0.25

Goals: Keep the credit in premium received from selling the multiple short puts when this strategy is entered. A drop in the price of the underlying moves the long puts deeper ITM for an increase in premium value and makes this trade even more profitable.

Manage: If the long put moves deeper ITM from a drop in the price of the underlying security, or even if a price rally occurs, the premium collected when this trade is entered is retained. If the price of the underlying drops to the strike of the multiple short puts, close the trade for the profit near the peak of the risk profile's plotline for the maximum achievable profit. If the price drop exceeds the strike of the short put options, close the trade before it begins to lose premium.

Profit: Close when this trade returns a profit that is greater than or equal to 30 percent.

Loss: This trade is subject to a loss if retained during a strong drop in the price of the underlying. Close this trade when the underlying is close to the strike of the OTM short puts to avoid a loss.

Equity Collar

Strategy: Sell *n* ATM or Slightly OTM Puts, ≤ 56 DTE
Buy *n* ATM Puts, Same Expiry
Buy or Own *n* × 100 Shares

Example:

Strategy	Buy/ Sell	Qty	Symbol	Trade Date	Exp. Date	Strike	Type	Price
Equity Collar	SELL	−5	X	02/05/18	5/25/18	$32.50	CALL	−$1.42
	BUY	+5	X	02/05/18	5/25/18	$32.00	PUT	$1.40
	BUY/ OWN	1,000	X				STOCK	$32.25

Bias: Bearish * Risk: Low * Reward: Low

Equity Collar Risk Profile

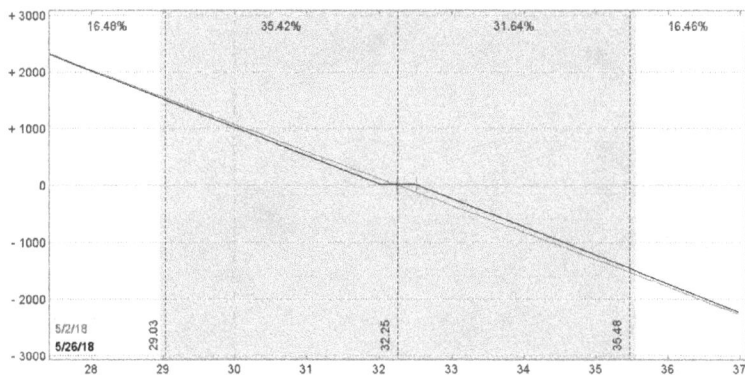

Price Chart: Downtrending off of resistance

Current IV%: ≈ 20%

IV Rank: ≈ 30

Trade: Buy one ATM put option for each 100 shares of owned stock; sell an equivalent number of slightly OTM call options to offset the cost of the long put options.

Typical Strike Deltas:

   Long Puts ≈ −0.50 to −0.45

   Short Calls ≈ −0.50 to −0.45

Goals: The long put options serve as a hedge against a drop in the price of the stock by moving deeper ITM. The long call is sold to offset the cost of the long put. The owned stock covers the short call options in case of a price rally.

Manage: If the long put moves deeper ITM from a drop in the price of the underlying security, a portion of the stock's reduction in value is offset by the drop in the value of the short calls. If the stock price continues to drop and the contracts are close to expiration, the long put options can be exercised to recover from the drop in the price of the stock. This transaction would normally be auto-exercised at option expiration. When exercised, the stock is delivered to a short put seller who must pay $32 per share, that is, the strike of the long put. In addition, the premium of the short call will have dropped in value. This permits the trader to buy to close the short call options for less than originally received. Or, more likely and when close to option expiration, the short calls may simply expire worthless, which permits the trader to retain all of the premium received when the short calls were initially sold.

If the stock rallies in opposition to the trader's bearish bias, the long put is sold for what premium remains. The short call would be bought and the trader would either keep the stock or sell it when a suitable profit is available.

Profit: Hedging strategies are used to limit losses rather than for profit. However, if the hedged stock experiences a strong price rally, the stock's profit could partially offset the difference in option premium initially paid when the long put and short call were bought.

Loss: This trade is subject to a loss if retained during a strong rally in the price of the underlying stock.

Protective Call

Strategy: Buy n ATM Calls, ≥ 90 DTE
Short n × 100 Shares

Example:

Strategy	Buy/ Sell	Qty	Symbol	Trade Date	Exp. Date	Strike	Type	Price
Protective Call	BUY	+5	EXAS	09/07/17	01/19/18	$45.00	CALL	−$4.30
	SHORT	−500	EXAS	09/07/17			STOCK	$43.20

Bias: Bearish * Risk: High * Reward: Low

Protective Call Risk Profile

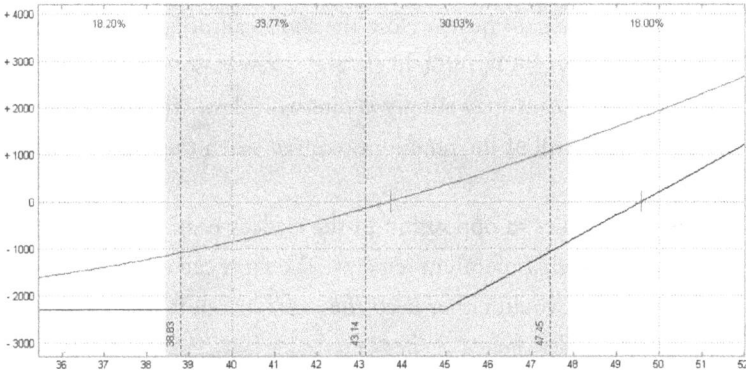

Price Chart: Downtrending off of resistance

Current IV%: ≤ 20%

IV Rank: ≤ 30

Trade: Buy *n* ATM call options.

Typical Strike Delta:

   Long Calls ≈ −0.50 to −0.45

Goals: Hedge the value of a short stock position held in the trader's account when the market rallies contrary to a trader's bearish bias.

Manage: If a rally in the price of the underlying security occurs, the long call option moves deeper ITM and offsets a portion of the trader's short stock value. If a protective stop is placed at a price above the short stock position (see Loss in the following paragraphs) and the price of the underlying experiences a strong rally, the short stock would be closed and the protective call could return a profit as it moves deeper ITM, although this is not the original intention of a protective call.

Profit: Hedging strategies are intended to partially offset a loss for risk management and are not intended to return a profit.

Loss: The protective call partially offsets a loss in the price of the shorted stock. Note that a conditional protective stop order could also be added a few dollars above the entry price of the short stock to limit the loss.

Long Call Butterfly (Balanced)

Strategy: Buy n ITM Calls, $\leq$ 14 DTE

Sell $2n$ ATM or Slightly OTM Calls, Same Expiry

Buy n OTM Calls, Higher Strike, Same Expiry

(Same Width Between Strikes)

Example:

Strategy	Buy/ Sell	Qty	Symbol	Trade Date	Exp. Date	Strike	Type	Price
Long Call Butterfly	BUY	+5	EXAS	07/18/17	08/18/17	$38.00	CALL	−$3.55
	SELL	−10	EXAS	07/18/17	08/18/17	$39.00	CALL	$2.98
	BUY	+5	EXAS	07/18/17	08/18/17	$40.00	CALL	−$2.53

Bias: Bullish * Risk: Low * Reward: Low

Long Call Butterfly (Balanced) Risk Profile

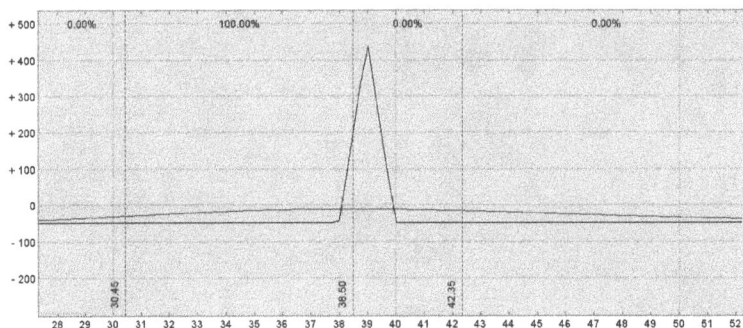

Price Chart: Uptrending

Current IV%: ≈ 50%

IV Rank: ≈ 50

Trade: Buy n ITM call options; sell $2n$ ATM call options; buy n OTM call options.

Typical Strike Deltas:

Lower Long Calls ≈ 0.55 to 0.50

Central Short Calls ≈ −0.50 to −0.45

Higher Long Calls ≈ 0.45 to 0.40

NOTE: The number of long option contracts used in the outside options, referred to as the *wings*, MUST be equal to the number of short contracts used in the center options, referred to as the *body*. (Although these long call butterflies typically straddle the ATM strike, both long and short butterflies are often placed entirely ITM or OTM. Long butterflies are more popular than short butterflies as they are typically more successful.)

Butterfly Type	Description
Balanced butterflies	Same number of option contracts in each wing (2/4/2).
Unbalanced butterflies	Different number of option contracts in each wing (1/4/3).
Traditional butterflies	Identical strike widths between butterfly wings and body. Bullish long call butterfly body often placed slightly OTM; bearish long put butterfly body often placed slightly OTM.
Broken wing butterflies	Different strike widths between butterfly wings and body.
Unbalanced broken wing butterflies	Different strike widths between butterfly wings and body and different number of option contracts in each wing.

Goals: When bullish, place the strikes of the butterfly to profit from a rally in the price of the underlying. The short butterfly body is typically placed at the trader's target price. Butterflies are defined-risk strategies. Losses are limited when a strong move in the price of the underlying occurs. This is verifiable by looking at accompanying risk profiles.

Manage: Close the butterfly for profit if and when the price of the underlying rises above the zero line and shows profit. Butterfly spreads are usually closed with several days remaining till expiration—typically 25 percent of the time remaining till expiration. This minimizes *gamma risk*, which occurs as the options approach expiration. Butterflies are rarely closed at or near the peak of the plot, referred to as the *witch's hat* or *tent*.

Profit: Close when this trade returns a profit of 15 to 20 percent.

Loss: This trade experiences a limited loss that rarely exceeds 20 percent.

DO NOT PERMIT OPTIONS TO EXPIRE ITM!

Short Call Butterfly (Balanced)

Strategy: Sell n ITM Calls, ≤ 14 DTE

Buy 2n ATM or Slightly ITM Calls, Higher Strike, Same Expiry

Sell n OTM Calls, Same Expiry

(Same Width Between Strikes)

Example:

Strategy	Buy/ Sell	Qty	Symbol	Trade Date	Exp. Date	Strike	Type	Price
Short Call Butterfly	SELL	−5	EXAS	07/18/17	8/18/17	$36.00	CALL	$4.75
	BUY	+10	EXAS	07/18/17	8/18/17	$39.00	CALL	−$2.98
	SELL	−5	EXAS	07/18/17	8/18/17	$42.00	CALL	$1.73

Bias: Bullish or Bearish * Risk: Low * Reward: Low

Short Call Butterfly (Balanced) Risk Profile

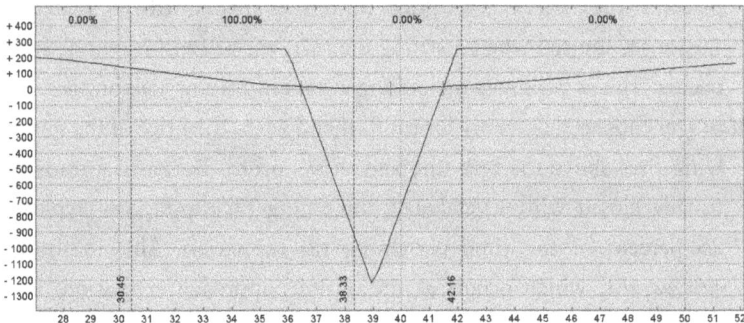

Price Chart: Strong directional price breakouts

Current IV%: ≈ 50%

IV Rank: ≈ 50

Trade: Sell *n* ITM call options; buy *2n* ATM call options; sell *n* OTM call options.

Typical Strike Deltas:

Lower Short Calls ≈ −0.50 to −0.55

Central Long Calls ≈ 0.50 to 0.45

Higher Short Calls ≈ −0.45 to −0.40

NOTE: Long butterflies that include long wing options and short body options are more popular than short butterfly options. Short call and put butterflies are included for comparison purposes. (See the long call butterfly's note and table for more information.)

Goals: This trade requires a strong directional price breakout, and even then, this strategy cannot succeed without careful trade management.

Manage: This trade requires careful management and would rarely be left in its original form, which is a losing trade. Instead, it would more likely be legged into a vertical call on the basis of the underlying's directional price move. If the central long calls of the body move ITM, one or both of the short call wings are closed.

Profit: Close losing short positions; sell the long calls when this trade returns a profit of 15 to 20 percent.

Loss: A debit is required when entering this trade. It will suffer a loss unless it is converted to either a vertical call spread or an ITM long call. Many traders avoid short call and short put butterflies. **DO NOT PERMIT OPTIONS TO EXPIRE ITM!**

Long Put Butterfly (Balanced)

Strategy: Buy n ITM Puts, ≤ 14 DTE

Sell 2n ATM or Slightly OTM Puts, Same Expiry

Buy n OTM Puts, Lower Strike, Same Expiry

(Same Width Between Strikes)

Example:

Strategy	Buy/ Sell	Qty	Symbol	Trade Date	Exp. Date	Strike	Type	Price
Long Put Butterfly	BUY	+5	TSLA	07/18/17	8/18/17	$315.00	PUT	−$13.10
	SELL	−10	TSLA	07/18/17	8/18/17	$320.00	PUT	$15.25
	BUY	+5	TSLA	07/18/17	8/18/17	$325.00	PUT	−$17.63

Bias: Bearish * Risk: Low * Reward: Low

Long Put Butterfly (Balanced) Risk Profile

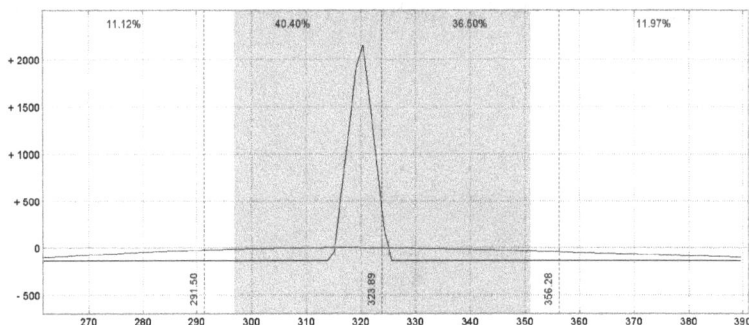

Price Chart: Downtrending

Current IV%: ≈ 50%

IV Rank: ≈ 50

Trade: Buy *n* ITM put options; buy 2*n* ATM put options; sell *n* OTM put options.

Typical Strike Deltas:

Lower Long Puts ≈ ≥ −0.47 to −0.45

Central Short Puts ≈ 0.48 to 0.45

Higher Long Puts ≈ −0.50 to −0.55

NOTE: Long butterflies that include long wing options and short body options are more popular than short butterfly options. Short call and put butterflies are included for comparison purposes. (See the long call butterfly's note and table for more information.)

Goals: This trade relies on a drop in the price of the underlying security. Place the strikes of the butterfly to profit from a drop in the price of the underlying. The butterfly is a defined-risk strategy. Losses are limited when a strong rally in the price of the underlying occurs.

Manage: Close the butterfly several days prior to expiration before *gamma risk* begins to "whipsaw" premium value. Be ready to close this trade quickly when the price is in the bottom one-third of the witch's hat of the risk profile.

Profit: Close when this trade returns a profit of 15 to 20 percent.

Loss: This trade experiences a limited loss that rarely exceeds 20 percent.

DO NOT PERMIT OPTIONS TO EXPIRE ITM!

Short Put Butterfly (Balanced)

Strategy: Sell n ITM Puts, $\leq$ 14 DTE

Buy $2n$ ATM or Slightly OTM Puts, Same Expiry

Sell n OTM Puts, Same Expiry,

(Same Width Between Strikes)

Example:

Strategy	Buy/ Sell	Qty	Symbol	Trade Date	Exp. Date	Strike	Type	Price
Short Put Butterfly	SELL	−3	GM	11/09/17	11/17/17	$41.00	PUT	−$0.16
	BUY	+6	GM	11/09/17	11/17/17	$42.00	PUT	$0.46
	SELL	−3	GM	11/09/17	11/17/17	$43.00	PUT	−$1.08

Bias: Neutral * Risk: Low * Reward: Low

Short Put Butterfly Risk Profile

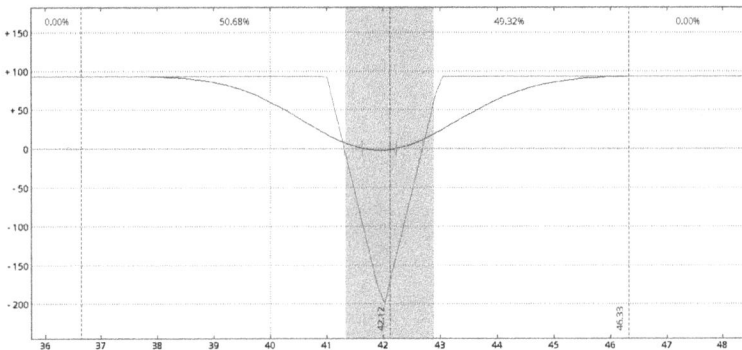

Price Chart: Strong directional price fluctuations

Current IV%: ≈ 50%

IV Rank: ≈ 50

Trade: Sell n ITM put options; buy $2n$ ATM put options; sell n OTM put options.

Typical Strike Deltas:

   Lower Short Puts ≈ 0.45 to 0.47

   Central Long Puts ≈ −0.48 to −0.52

   Higher Short Puts ≈ 0.52 to 0.55

NOTE: Long butterflies that include long wing options and short body options are more popular than short butterfly options. Short call and put butterflies are included for comparison purposes. (See the long call butterfly's note and table for more information.)

Goals: This trade requires a strong directional price breakout, and even then, this strategy cannot succeed without careful trade management.

Manage: This trade requires careful management and would rarely be left in its original form, which is potentially a losing trade. Instead, it would more likely be legged into a vertical put on the basis of the underlying's directional price move. If the central long puts of the body move ITM, close one or both of the short put wings. (Remember, butterfly trades are typically closed when approximately 25 percent of the time till expiration remains.)

Profit: Close losing short positions; sell the long puts when this trade returns a profit of 15 to 20 percent.

Loss: A debit is required when entering this trade. It will suffer a loss unless it is legged into either a vertical put spread or an ITM long put. Many traders avoid short put and short call butterflies. **DO NOT PERMIT OPTIONS TO EXPIRE ITM!**

Long Call Butterfly (Unbalanced)

Strategy: Buy x ITM Calls, ≤ 14 DTE

Sell x + y ATM or Slightly OTM Calls, Same Expiry

Buy y OTM Calls, Higher Strike, Same Expiry,

(Same Width Between Strikes)

Example:

Strategy	Buy/ Sell	Qty	Symbol	Trade Date	Exp. Date	Strike	Type	Price
Unbalanced Long Call Butterfly	BUY	+2	FDX	11/09/17	11/17/17	$215	CALL	−3.90
	SELL	−6	FDX	11/09/17	11/17/17	$220	CALL	$1.24
	BUY	+4	FDX	11/09/17	11/17/17	$225	CALL	$0.23

Bias: Bullish * Risk: Low * Reward: Low

Unbalanced Long Call Butterfly (Unbalanced) Risk Profile

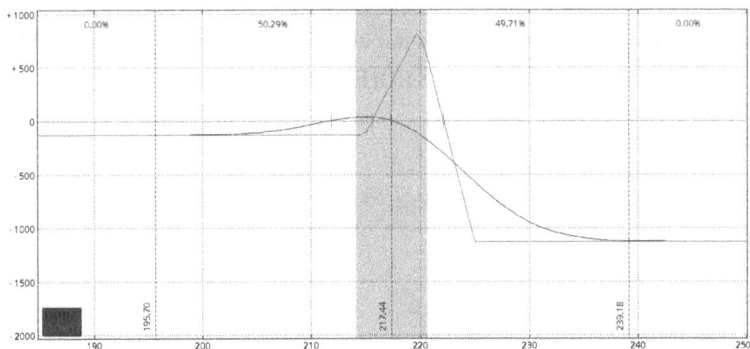

Price Chart: Uptrending

Current IV%: ≈ 50%

IV Rank: ≈ 50

Trade: Buy x ITM call options; buy x + y ATM call options; sell y OTM call options.

Typical Strike Deltas:

   Lower Long Calls ≈ 0.45 to 0.50

   Central Short Calls ≈ −0.50 to −0.45

   Higher Long Calls ≈ 0.48 to 0.40

NOTE: Long butterflies that include long wing options and short body options are more popular than short butterfly options. Short call and put butterflies are included for comparison purposes. (See the long call butterfly's note and table for more information.)

Goals: When bullish, place the strikes of the butterfly to profit from a rally in the price of the underlying. Adjust the strike widths to control the entry debit or credit amount and profit potential. Examine different setups on risk profiles. Enter the trade when satisfied that the plot fits your market bias. Losses are limited even if the price of the underlying drops.

Manage: As shown on the risk profile, careful trade management is important. Although the profit potential may be greater than with a balanced butterfly, the risk is also increased. To profit, this butterfly strategy must be closed if and when the price of the underlying is in the bottom one-third of the *witch's hat* of the risk profile's plotline. Remember, butterflies are typically closed when approximately 25 percent of the time remaining till expiration exists and before *gamma risk* becomes a factor.

Profit: Close when this trade returns a profit of 15 to 20 percent.

Loss: This trade experiences a limited loss that rarely exceeds 20 percent.

DO NOT PERMIT OPTIONS TO EXPIRE ITM!

Short Call Butterfly (Unbalanced)

Strategy: Sell *x* ITM Calls, Expire ≤ 14 DTE

Buy *x* + *y* ATM Calls, Same Expiry

Sell *y* OTM Calls, Same Expiry

(Same Width Between Strikes)

Example:

Strategy	Buy/ Sell	Qty	Symbol	Trade Date	Exp. Date	Strike	Type	Price
Unbalanced Short Call Butterfly	SELL	−3	AAPL	7/20/17	8/04/17	$150.00	CALL	$3.40
	BUY	+10	AAPL	7/20/17	8/04/17	$152.50	CALL	−$2.27
	SELL	−7	AAPL	7/20/17	8/04/17	$155.00	CALL	$1.44

Bias: Bullish * Risk: Low * Reward: Low

Short Call Butterfly Risk Profile (Unbalanced)

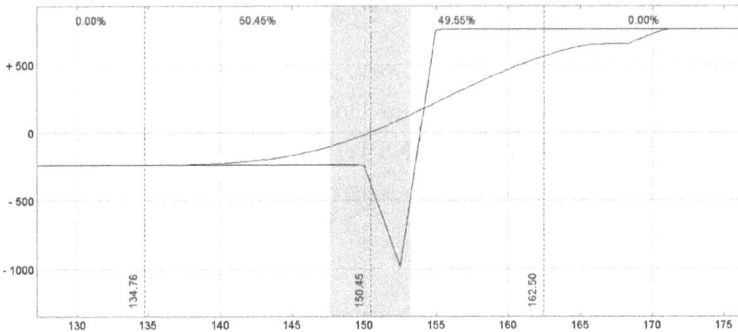

Price Chart: Uptrending

Current IV%: ≈ 50%

IV Rank: ≈ 50

Trade: Sell *x* ITM call options; buy *x* + *y* ATM call options; sell *y* OTM call options.

Typical Strike Deltas:

Lower Short Calls ≈ −0.60 to −0.50

Central Long Calls ≈ 0.50 to 0.45

Higher Short Calls ≈ −0.45 to −0.40

NOTE: Long butterflies that include long wing options and short body options are more popular than short butterfly options. Short call and put butterflies are included for comparison purposes. (See the long call butterfly's note and table for more information.)

Goals: This trade requires the price of the underlying security to rally to return a profit, as indicated by this strategy's risk profile. This might encourage the trader to choose a slightly longer time till expiration to provide ample time for the price to rally for a profitable outcome.

Manage: As described in the previous paragraph, a price rally above $5 per share rewards the trade, which would likely be closed as soon as it returns an acceptable profit (see the above-mentioned risk profile). A rally increases the premium values of the long call positions. The short call wings would be closed, while the central long calls of the body would be monitored until closed for the increased premium. As noted earlier, short butterfly trades are inferior to the long call butterfly trades, which carry less risk and are easier to manage.

Profit: Close losing short positions; sell the long calls when this trade returns a profit of 15 to 20 percent.

Loss: A debit is required to enter this trade. It will suffer a loss unless it is legged into either a vertical call spread or an ITM long call. Many traders avoid short call and short put butterflies. **DO NOT PERMIT OPTIONS TO EXPIRE ITM!**

Long Put Butterfly (Unbalanced)

Strategy: Buy x ITM Puts, ≤ 14 DTE

Sell x + y ATM Puts, Same Expiry

Buy y OTM Puts, Same Expiry

(Same Width Between Strikes)

Example:

Strategy	Buy/ Sell	Qty	Symbol	Trade Date	Exp. Date	Strike	Type	Price
Unbalanced Long Put Butterfly	BUY	+8	MSFT	08/15/17	09/01/17	$73.00	PUT	−$0.88
	SELL	−10	MSFT	08/15/17	09/01/17	$73.50	PUT	$1.10
	BUY	+2	MSFT	08/15/17	09/01/17	$74.00	PUT	−$1.37

Bias: Bullish * Risk: Low * Reward: Low

Long Put Butterfly Risk Profile (Unbalanced)

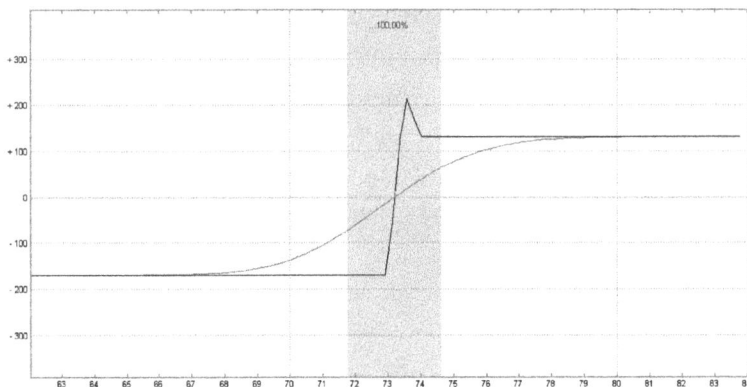

Price Chart: Uptrending

Current IV%: ≈ 50%

IV Rank: ≈ 50

Trade: Buy x ITM put options; sell x + y ATM put options; buy y OTM put options, same strike widths

Typical Strike Deltas:

   Lower Long Puts ≈ −0.45 to −0.47

   Central Short Puts ≈ 0.48 to 0.50

   Higher Long Puts ≈ −0.50 to −0.55

NOTE: Long butterflies that include long wing options and short body options are more popular than short butterfly options. Short call and put butterflies are included for comparison purposes. (See the long call butterfly's note and table for more information.)

Goals: It is possible to structure this defined-risk bullish butterfly to fit either a bearish or bullish bias. The example is bullish. (A bearish bias buys more ITM puts above than OTM puts below, which changes the risk graph accordingly.) Unbalanced and broken wing butterflies increase both profit potential and risk, which always go hand in hand.

Manage: Close the butterfly for profit if and when the price of the underlying is in the bottom one-third of the peak of the risk profile's plotline, that is, the peak of the *witch's hat*. If the price experiences a drop rather than a rally, sell the long puts and keep the short puts. The short puts can either be closed for a profit or allowed to expire worthless.

Profit: Close when this trade returns a profit of 15 to 20 percent.

Loss: This trade experiences a limited loss of rarely more than 25 percent when properly configured. **DO NOT PERMIT OPTIONS TO EXPIRE ITM!**

Short Put Butterfly (Unbalanced)
Strategy: Sell x ITM Puts, ≤ 14 DTE
Buy x + y ATM Puts, Same Expiry
Sell y OTM Puts, Same Expiry
(Same Width Between Strikes)

Example:

Strategy	Buy/ Sell	Qty	Symbol	Trade Date	Exp. Date	Strike	Type	Price
Unbalanced	SELL	−3	TSLA	07/18/17	7/28/17	$325.00	PUT	$6.75
Short Put	BUY	+10	TSLA	07/18/17	7/28/17	$327.50	PUT	−$7.83
Butterfly	SELL	−7	TSLA	07/18/17	7/28/17	$330.00	PUT	$9.08

Bias: Bullish * Risk: Low * Reward: Low

Short Put Butterfly Risk Profile (Unbalanced)

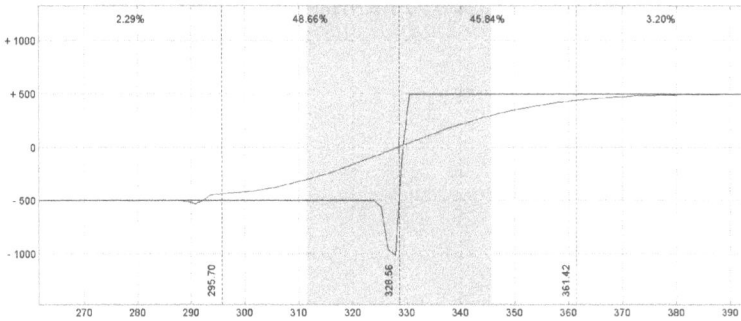

Price Chart: Uptrending

Current IV%: ≈ 50%

IV Rank: ≈ 50

Trade: Sell x ITM put options; buy $x + y$ ATM put options; sell y OTM put options, same strike widths. Also recall how short butterflies are less popular than long butterflies, where *long* designates either long call or long put butterfly wings.

Typical Strike Deltas:
   Lower Short Puts ≈ 0.45 to 0.40
   Central Long Puts ≈ −0.45 to −0.50
   Higher Short Puts ≈ 0.50 to 0.55

NOTE: Long butterflies that include long wing options and short body options are more popular than short butterfly options. Short call and put butterflies are included for comparison purposes. (See the long call butterfly's note and table for more information.)

Goals: This defined-risk bullish butterfly strategy can be structured to fit either bearish or bullish bias by reversing the number of option contracts sold in the wings. The example is bullish. (A bearish bias sells more OTM puts below than OTM puts above, which changes the risk graph accordingly.)

Manage: Close the butterfly for profit as soon as the price of the underlying exceeds $332. If the price experiences a drop rather than a rally, close the trade to recover the premium that remains in the 10 long call options.

Profit: Close when this trade returns a profit of 15 to 20 percent.

Loss: This trade experiences a limited loss that rarely exceeds 25 percent when properly configured. **DO NOT PERMIT OPTIONS TO EXPIRE ITM!**

Broken Wing Long Call Butterfly

Strategy: Buy *n* ITM Calls, ≤ 14 DTE

Sell 2*n* ATM Calls, Same Expiry

Buy *n* OTM Calls, Same Expiry

(Different Width Between Strikes)

Example:

Strategy	Buy/ Sell	Qty	Symbol	Trade Date	Exp. Date	Strike	Type	Price
Broken	BUY	+5	FDX	08/15/17	9/01/17	$207.50	CALL	−$3.12
Wing Long Call	SELL	−10	FDX	08/15/17	9/01/17	$210.00	CALL	$1.89
Butterfly	BUY	+5	FDX	08/15/17	9/01/17	$215.00	CALL	−$0.53

Bias: Neutral * Risk: Low * Reward: Low

Broken Wing Long Call Butterfly Risk Profile

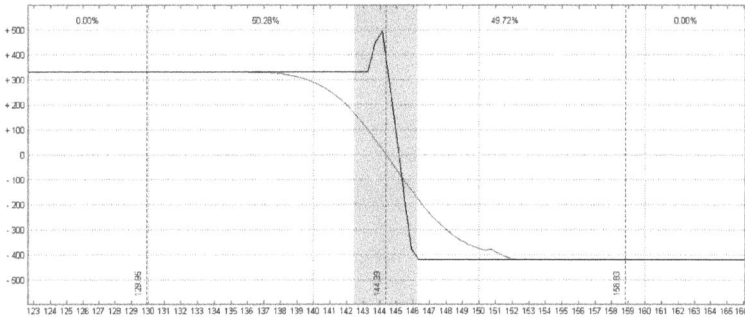

Price Chart: Downtrending

Current IV%: ≈ 50%

IV Rank: ≈ 50

Trade: Buy *x* ITM call options; sell *x* + *y* ATM call options; buy *y* OTM call options, different strike widths.

Typical Strike Deltas:

   Lower Long Calls ≈ 0.45 to 0.50

   Central Short Calls ≈ −0.50 to −0.45

   Higher Long Calls ≈ 0.48 to 0.40

NOTE: Long butterflies that include long wing options and short body options are more popular than short butterfly options. Short call and put butterflies are included for comparison purposes. (See the long call butterfly's note and table for more information.)

Goals: When bearish, the example trade places the strikes of the butterfly's long option wing and short option body to profit from a drop in the price of the underlying. Adjust the strike widths to control the entry debit or credit amount. Examine different setups on risk profiles. Enter the trade when satisfied that the plot fits your market bias. Losses are limited even if the price of the underlying rallies.

Manage: As shown on the risk profile, careful trade management is important. To profit, this butterfly strategy must be closed if and when the price of the underlying drops below $145 as shown by the plot within the risk profile.

Profit: Close when this trade returns a profit that is greater than or equal to 15 to 20 percent.

Loss: This trade experiences a limited loss that rarely exceeds 20 percent. **DO NOT PERMIT OPTIONS TO EXPIRE ITM!**

Broken Wing Short Call Butterfly
Strategy: Sell n ITM Calls, $\leq$ 14 DTE
Buy $2n$ ATM Calls, Same Expiry
Sell n OTM Calls, Same Expiry
(Different Width Between Strikes)

Example:

Strategy	Buy/ Sell	Qty	Symbol	Trade Date	Exp. Date	Strike	Type	Price
Broken	SELL	−5	WMT	07/18/17	7/28/17	$75.00	CALL	$1.50
Wing Short Call	BUY	+10	WMT	07/18/17	7/28/17	$76.50	CALL	−$0.57
Butterfly	SELL	−5	WMT	07/18/17	7/28/17	$77.50	CALL	$0.24

Bias: Bullish or Bearish * Risk: Low * Reward: Low

Broken Wing Short Call Butterfly Risk Profile

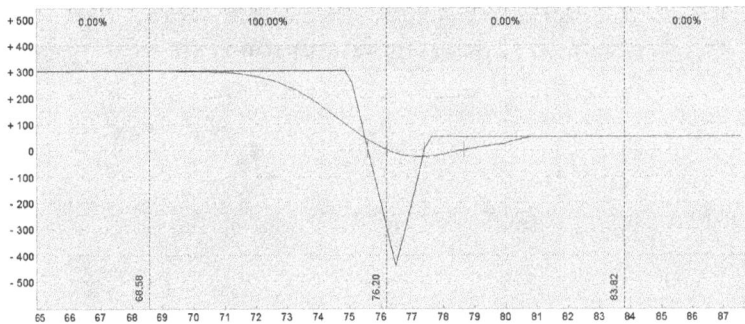

Price Chart: Downtrending
Current IV%: ≈ 50%
IV Rank: ≈ 50
Trade: Sell x ITM call options; buy $x + y$ ATM call options; sell y OTM call options, different strike widths.
Typical Strike Deltas:
    Lower Short Calls ≈ −0.58 to −0.52
    Central Long Calls ≈ 0.51 to −0.48
    Higher Short Calls ≈ −0.48 to −0.40

NOTE: Long butterflies that include long wing options and short body options are more popular than short butterfly options. Short call and put butterflies are included for comparison purposes. (See the long call butterfly's note and table for more information.)

Goals: When bearish, place the strikes of the butterfly to profit from a drop in the price of the underlying. Adjust the strike widths to control the entry debit or credit amount. Examine different setups on risk profiles. Enter the trade when satisfied that the plot fits your market bias. Losses are limited even if the price of the underlying rallies.

Manage: As shown on the risk profile, careful trade management is important. To profit, this butterfly strategy must be closed if and when the price of the underlying drops below $75 as shown by the risk profile's plotline. OTM broken wing unbalanced butterflies are among some of the most popular butterflies traded because they are profitable when they expire OTM.

Profit: Close when this trade returns a profit of 15 to 20 percent.

Loss: This trade experiences a limited loss that rarely exceeds 20 percent.

DO NOT PERMIT OPTIONS TO EXPIRE ITM!

Broken Wing Long Put Butterfly

Strategy: Buy *n* ITM Puts, ≤ 14 DTE

Sell 2*n* ATM Puts, Same Expiry

Buy *n* OTM Puts, Same Expiry

(Different Width Between Strikes)

Example:

Strategy	Buy/ Sell	Qty	Symbol	Trade Date	Exp. Date	Strike	Type	Price
Broken Wing Long Put Butterfly	BUY	+5	WMT	08/20/17	09/01/17	$78.00	PUT	−$0.48
	SELL	−10	WMT	08/20/17	09/01/17	$79.00	PUT	$0.78
	BUY	+5	WMT	08/20/17	09/01/17	$79.50	PUT	−$1.00

Bias: Bullish * Risk: Low * Reward: Low

Broken Wing Long Put Butterfly Risk Profile

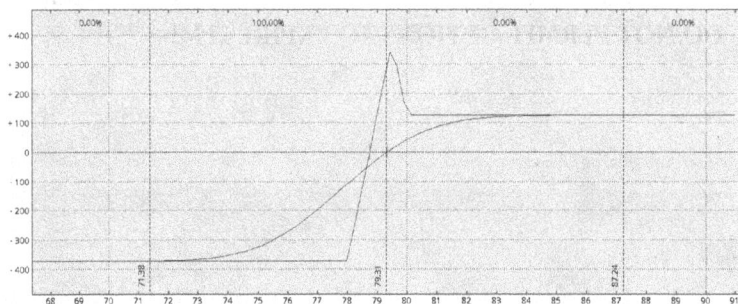

Price Chart: Uptrending

Current IV%: ≈ 50%

IV Rank: ≈ 50

Trade: Buy *x* ITM put options; sell *x* + *y* ATM put options; buy *y* OTM put options, different strike widths

Typical Strike Deltas:

Lower Long Puts ≈ −0.45 to −0.47

Central Short Puts ≈ 0.48 to 0.50

Higher Long Puts ≈ −0.50 to −0.55

NOTE: Long butterflies that include long wing options and short body options are more popular than short butterfly options. Short call and put butterflies are included for comparison purposes. (See the long call butterfly's note and table for more information.)

Goals: It is possible to structure this defined-risk bullish butterfly strategy to fit either a bearish or bullish bias. As seen on the risk profile, the example is bullish. (A bearish bias buys more ITM puts above than OTM puts below, which changes the risk graph accordingly.)

Manage: Close the butterfly for profit if the price of the underlying rallies above $79.50 to $80. If the price experiences a drop rather than a rally, sell the long puts and keep the short puts. The short puts can either be closed for a profit or left to expire worthless.

Profit: Close when this trade returns a profit of 15 to 20 percent.

Loss: This trade experiences a limited loss that rarely exceeds 25 percent when properly configured. **DO NOT PERMIT OPTIONS TO EXPIRE ITM!**

Broken Wing Short Put Butterfly

Strategy: Sell n ITM Puts, $\leq$ 14 DTE

Buy $2n$ ATM Puts, Same Expiry

Sell n OTM Puts, Same Expiry

(Different Width Between Strikes)

Example:

Strategy	Buy/ Sell	Qty	Symbol	Trade Date	Exp. Date	Strike	Type	Price
Broken	SELL	−5	WMT	07/18/17	7/28/17	$75.00	PUT	$0.28
Wing Short Put	BUY	+10	WMT	07/18/17	7/28/17	$76.50	PUT	−$0.83
Butterfly	SELL	−5	WMT	07/18/17	7/28/17	$77.00	PUT	$1.14

Bias: Bearish * Risk: Low * Reward: Low

Broken Wing Short Put Butterfly Risk Profile

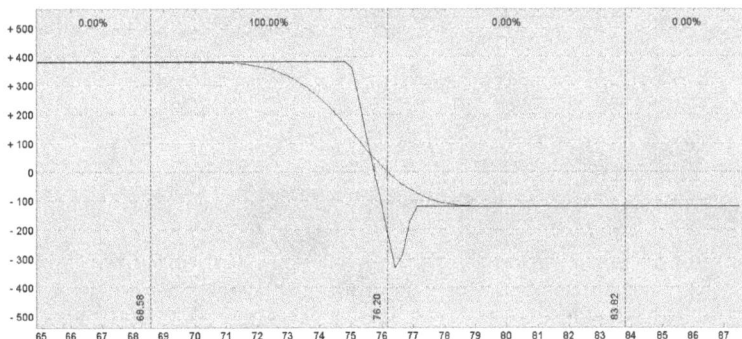

Price Chart: Downtrending

Current IV%: ≈ 50%

IV Rank: ≈ 50

Trade: Sell x ITM put options; buy $x + y$ ATM put options; sell y OTM put options, different strike widths.

Typical Strike Deltas:

Lower Short Puts ≈ 0.45 to 0.40

Central Long Puts ≈ −0.45 to −0.50

Higher Short Puts ≈ 0.50 to 0.55

NOTE: Long butterflies that include long wing options and short body options are more popular than short butterfly options. Short call and put butterflies are included for comparison purposes. (See the long call butterfly's note and table for more information.)

Goals: It's possible to structure this defined-risk butterfly strategy to fit either a bearish or bullish bias by reversing the number of option contracts sold in the wings. The example is bearish. (A bearish bias sells OTM puts that are closer to the ATM strike for less premium than received by selling the ITM options.)

Manage: Recall how both unbalanced and broken wing butterflies increase both profit potential and risk. Close the butterfly for profit as soon as the price drop of the underlying drops to or below $75 on the X axis of the risk profile. If the price experiences a rally rather than a drop, close the trade to recover the premium that remains in the 10 long call options and keep the short $75 put until it can either be closed for profit or expires worthless.

Profit: Close when this trade returns a profit of 15 to 20 percent.

Loss: This trade experiences a limited loss that rarely exceeds 25 percent when properly configured. **DO NOT PERMIT OPTIONS TO EXPIRE ITM!**

Broken Wing Long Call Butterfly (Unbalanced)

Strategy: Buy x ITM Calls, ≤ 14 DTE
Sell x + y ATM or Slightly OTM Calls, Same Expiry
Buy y OTM Calls, Higher Strike, Same Expiry,
(Different Widths Between Strikes)

Example:

Strategy	Buy/ Sell	Qty	Symbol	Trade Date	Exp. Date	Strike	Type	Price
Unbalanced Long Call Butterfly	BUY	+3	FDX	11/09/17	11/17/17	$165	CALL	−$0.895
	SELL	−10	FDX	11/09/17	11/17/17	$167.5	CALL	$0.60
	BUY	+7	FDX	11/09/17	11/17/17	$172.5	CALL	−$0.305

Bias: Bullish or Bearish * Risk: Moderate * Reward: Low

Broken Wing Long Call Butterfly (Unbalanced) Risk Profile

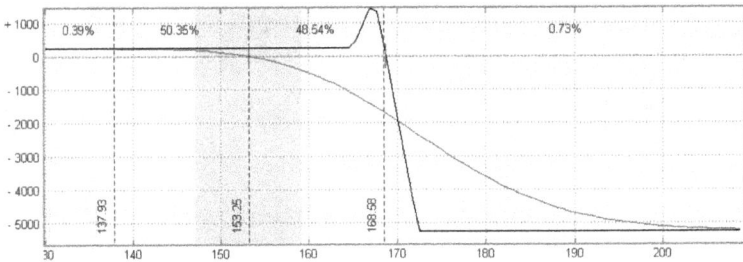

Price Chart: Up-trending

Current IV%: ≈ 50%

IV Rank: ≈ 50

Trade: Buy x ITM call options; buy x + y ATM call options; sell y OTM call options, different strike widths.

Typical Strike Deltas:

Lower Long Calls ≈ 0.20 to 0.30

Central Short Calls ≈ −0.18 to −0.25

Higher Long Calls ≈ 0.10 to 0.20

NOTE: Long butterflies that include long wing options and short body options are more popular than short butterfly options. Short call and put butterflies are included for comparison purposes. (See the long call butterfly's note and table for more information.)

Goals: When bullish or neutral, place the strikes of the butterfly to profit from a rally in the price of the underlying. If the price of the underlying drops, keep the credit received when opened. Examine different strike and long option value setups on risk profiles. The one shown illustrates an entry credit, making this a popular strategy. Enter the trade when satisfied that the plot fits your market bias.

Manage: As shown on the risk profile, a rally requires careful trade management. This butterfly strategy can be closed for profit when the price of the underlying moves into the tent to return a profit between 15 to 20 percent. If the price fails to rally or drops and the strikes remain OTM, you can let the trade expire worthless to avoid commissions and exchange fees. Consider entering a Mark-triggered alert if the price of FDX breaches $165.

Profit: Close when this trade returns a profit of close to $500; as can be seen, a strong rally can return even more.

Loss: If unmanaged, a strong FDX price rally risks a loss in excess of $5,000. **DO NOT PERMIT OPTIONS TO EXPIRE ITM!**

2-Step Long Call Butterfly

Strategy: Combines Two Vertical Calls Entered at Different Times.

1st Trade: Buy *n* ATM Calls, ≤ 21 DTE

Sell *n* OTM Calls, Same Expiry

2nd Trade: Sell *n* OTM Calls, Same Strike As 1st Short Call, ≤ 14 DTE

Buy *n* OTM Calls, Same Expiry, Higher Strike to Create a Butterfly.

Example:

Strategy	Buy/ Sell	Qty	Symbol	Trade Date	Exp. Date	Strike	Type	Price
2-Step Long Call Butterfly	BUY	+5	SPY	07/26/17	09/01/17	$244.00	CALL	−$1.47
	SELL	−5	SPY	07/26/17	09/01/17	$246.00	CALL	$0.78
	SELL	−5	SPY	07/26/17	09/15/17	$246.00	CALL	$0.91
	BUY	+5	SPY	07/26/17	09/15/17	$248.00	CALL	−$0.57

Bias: Bullish or Bearish * Risk: Low * Reward: Low

2-Step Long Call Butterfly Risk Profile

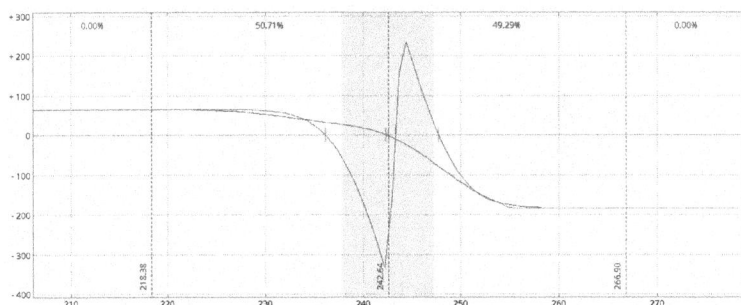

Price Chart: Uptrending preferred

Current IV%: ≈ 50%

IV Rank: ≈ 50

Trade: Buy *n* ATM call options, sell *n* OTM call options to create a bull call. Then "leg into" a bear call comprised of a short call and a farther

OTM long call as a trade management strategy. An identical number of short calls is added at the same strike as that of the original short calls. The OTM long calls form the upper wing of the butterfly. This two-step butterfly is a common maintenance strategy used with bull calls. The second vertical spread is often added later in the day or several days apart. Also, sufficient time till expiration of the initial bull call must exist to permit the addition of the bear call.

Typical Strike Deltas:
  Lower Short Calls ≈ −0.55 to −0.50
  Central Long Calls ≈ 0.50 to 0.45
  Higher Short Calls ≈ −0.45 to −0.40

NOTE: Long butterflies that include long wing options and short body options are more popular than short butterfly options. Short call and put butterflies are included for comparison purposes. (See the long call butterfly's note and table for more information.)

Goals: When bullish, place the strikes of the butterfly to profit from a rally in the price of the underlying. The butterfly is a defined-risk strategy. As shown by the plotline within the above risk profile, this strategy can also return a small profit if the price of the underlying drops below $235.

Manage: Close the butterfly for profit if and when the price of the underlying rallies to approximately one-third up the risk profile's tent-shaped plotline. Because the peak of the sample trade is reasonably narrow, close attention is required. Also notice how a price drop that exceeds $6.00 also rewards the addition of the options that comprise the bear call.

Profit: Close when this trade returns a profit of between 10 and 15 percent.

Loss: This trade's maximum loss is limited to approximately $320. **DO NOT PERMIT OPTIONS TO EXPIRE ITM!**

2-Step Short Call Butterfly

Strategy: Combines Two Vertical Calls Entered at Different Times

1st Trade: Sell n ATM Calls, ≤ 21 DTE

Buy n OTM Calls, Same Expiry

2nd Trade: Buy n OTM Calls, Same Strike As 1st Long Call, ≤ 21 DTE

Sell n OTM Calls, Higher Strike to Create a Butterfly, Same Expiry

Example:

Strategy	Buy/ Sell	Qty	Symbol	Trade Date	Exp. Date	Strike	Type	Price
2-Step Short Call Butterfly	SELL	−5	QQQ	08/15/17	9/01/17	$140.50	CALL	$1.76
	BUY	+5	QQQ	08/15/17	9/01/17	$141.50	CALL	−$1.22
	BUY	+5	QQQ	08/21/17	9/08/17	$141.50	CALL	−$1.57
	SELL	−5	QQQ	08/21/17	9/08/17	$142.50	CALL	$1.10

Bias: Bullish or Bearish * Risk: Low * Reward: Low

2-Step Short Call Butterfly Risk Profile

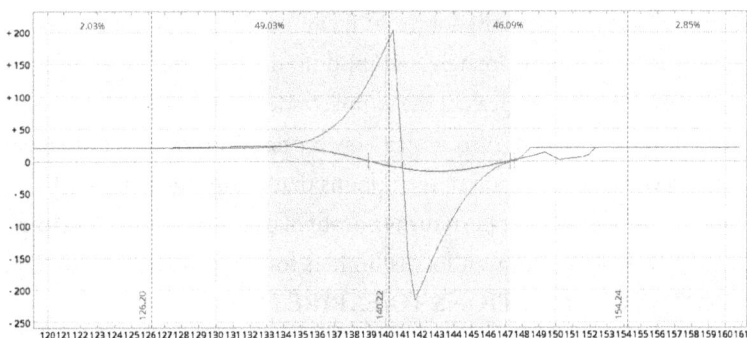

Price Chart: Unwanted price reversal when using a bear call

Current IV%: ≈ 50%

IV Rank: ≈ 50

Trade: Sell *n* ATM call options; buy *n* OTM call options to create a bear call. With ample time remaining till expiration, consider legging into a butterfly by overlaying a bull call so the combination creates a short call butterfly. The OTM short calls form the upper wing of the butterfly. This two-step butterfly is sometimes used as a maintenance strategy for a failing bear call spread.

Typical Strike Deltas:
   Lower Short Calls ≈ -0.50 to -0.55
   Central Long Calls ≈ 0.50 to 0.45
   Higher Short Calls ≈ -0.45 to -0.40

NOTE: Long butterflies that include long wing options and short body options are more popular than short butterfly options. Short call and put butterflies are included for comparison purposes. (See the long call butterfly's note and table for more information.)

Goals: This trade requires a directional price breakout, and even then, this strategy requires careful trade management. (Recall that long butterflies are typically superior to short butterflies.)

Manage: This trade benefits from a strong rally or a small drop to succeed. A $2.00 rally would result in the worst-case outcome, as shown in the preceding risk profile. The plotline also shows how either a price drop or a strong rally both have small profit potentials. The best outcome is for the underlying to be near $140 at either contract expiration or when the trade is closed.

Profit: Close this butterfly whenever it returns a small profit.

Loss: This trade's maximum loss is limited to approximately $220. **DO NOT PERMIT OPTIONS TO EXPIRE ITM!**

2-Step Long Put Butterfly

Strategy: Combines Two Vertical Calls Entered at Different Times

Strategy: 1st Trade: Buy n ATM Puts, ≤ 21 DTE

Sell n OTM Puts, Same Expiry

2nd Trade: Sell n OTM Puts (Same Strike As 1st Short Puts), ≤ 14 DTE

Buy n OTM Puts, Lower Strike to Create a Butterfly, Same Expiry

Example:

Strategy	Buy/ Sell	Qty	Symbol	Trade Date	Exp. Date	Strike	Type	Price
2-Step Long Put Butterfly	BUY	+5	SPY	07/26/17	8/04/17	$244.00	PUT	−$1.47
	SELL	−5	SPY	07/26/17	8/04/17	$246.00	PUT	$0.78
	SELL	−5	SPY	07/26/17	8/11/17	$246.00	PUT	$0.91
	BUY	+5	SPY	07/26/17	8/11/17	$248.00	PUT	−$0.57

Bias: Bearish * Risk: Low * Reward: Low

2-Step Long Put Butterfly Risk Profile

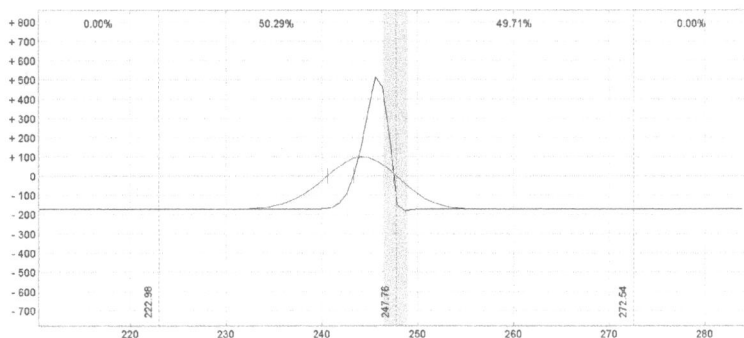

Price Chart: Unwanted price reversal (drop) when using a bull put

Current IV%: ≈ 50%

IV Rank: ≈ 50

Trade: Leg an existing bull put spread into a long put butterfly by buying n ATM put options and selling n OTM put options (a typical bear put vertical). An identical number of short puts is added at the same strike as that of the original short puts. The OTM long puts form the lower wing of the butterfly. Legging an existing bull put vertical into a long put butterfly is sometimes used to recover from a failing bull put vertical spread. Also, the initial bull put options must have ample time till expiration to permit the addition of the bear put.

Typical Strike Deltas:

   Lower Short Puts ≈ 0.45 to 0.50
   Central Long Puts ≈ −0.50 to −0.55
   Higher Short Puts ≈ 0.55 to 0.60

NOTE: Long butterflies that include long wing options and short body options are more popular than short butterfly options. Short call and put butterflies are included for comparison purposes. (See the long call butterfly's note and table for more information.)

Goals: When the price of the underlying begins to drop in opposition to the trader's bullish bias, the trade may be rescued (or the potential loss reduced) by legging the bull put vertical into a long put butterfly. Legging into a long put butterfly is rational because this butterfly offers a defined risk. As shown by the plotline in the above-mentioned risk profile, this strategy can also return a small profit if the price of the underlying becomes close to $245.

Manage: Close the butterfly for profit if and when the price of the underlying is within a few dollars of $245, or close the trade when the options are within 5 days of expiring.

Profit: Close when this trade returns a small profit approaching 10 percent, which may be a "best case outcome."

Loss: This trade's maximum loss is limited to approximately $185. **DO NOT PERMIT OPTIONS TO EXPIRE ITM!**

2-Step Short Put Butterfly

Strategy: Combines Two Vertical Call Trades Entered at
Different Times.

Strategy: 1st Trade: Sell n ATM Puts, ≤ 21 DTE

Buy n OTM Puts, Same Expiry

2nd Trade: Buy n OTM Puts (Same Strike As 1st Long Put),
≤ 14 DTE

Sell n OTM Puts, Higher Strike to Create a Butterfly, Same
Expiry

Example:

Strategy	Buy/ Sell	Qty	Symbol	Trade Date	Exp. Date	Strike	Type	Price
2-Step Short Put Butterfly	SELL	−5	AAPL	08/24/17	9/15/17	$160.00	PUT	$1.94
	BUY	+5	AAPL	08/24/17	9/15/17	$157.50	PUT	−$2.78
	BUY	+5	AAPL	08/24/17	9/22/17	$157.50	PUT	−$3.45
	SELL	−5	AAPL	08/24/17	9/22/17	$155.00	PUT	$4.58

Bias: Bearish * Risk: Low * Reward: Low

2-Step Short Put Butterfly Risk Profile

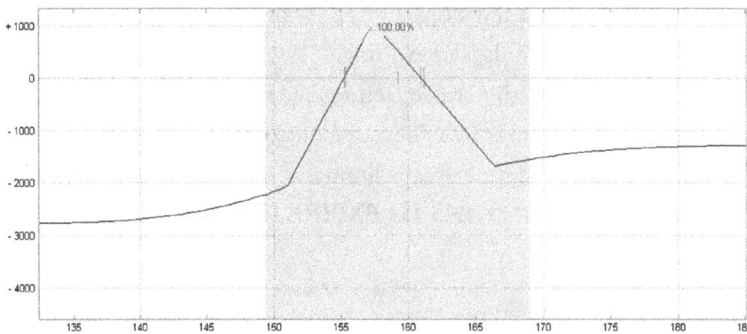

Price Chart: Unwanted price rally that threatens to defeat a working bear
put vertical spread

Current IV%: ≈ 50%

IV Rank: ≈ 50

Trade: Leg an existing bear put vertical into a short put butterfly by overlaying a bull put vertical. This could occur when the trader's bearish bias is wrong and the price of the underlying security rallies rather than dropping.

Typical Strike Deltas:
  Step 1 Short Puts ≈ 0.30 to 0.45
  Step 1 Long Puts ≈ −0.45 to −0.55
  Step 2 Long Puts ≈ −0.45 to −0.55
  Step 2 Short Puts ≈ 0.55 to 0.65

NOTE: Long butterflies that include long wing options and short body options are more popular than short butterfly options. Short call and put butterflies are included for comparison purposes. (See the long call butterfly's note and table for more information.)

Goals: This trade is used as a maintenance measure in order to offset a substantial loss from a strong price rally that opposes the trader's initial bearish bias.

Manage: A bull put vertical spread is legged into a failing bear put vertical spread to create a short put butterfly. The intent is to create a defined-risk butterfly to limit the loss potential that exists within the original bear put spread. However, as can quickly be seen on the risk profile, this conversion can be folly, as the short put butterfly now carries a potential loss of approximately $2,800. Therefore, once the resulting risk profile is examined, the trader would likely be better off simply closing the original bear put than legging it into a short put butterfly. Notice that a small profit range does exist either side of $157, but the likelihood of this occurring is small.

Profit: Close losing short positions and sell the long puts when this trade achieves either breakeven or a small profit or suffers a small loss.

Loss: This short put butterfly can potentially lose $2,800. The trader would likely close the original bear put vertical for a loss and move on.

DO NOT PERMIT OPTIONS TO EXPIRE ITM!

Double Butterfly

Strategy: Typically Traded on Weekly European-style Index Options (RUT, SPX, NDX); Combines Two Long Call or Long Put Butterfly Trades That Expire Simultaneously Inside 8 to 10 Days; Typically Balanced, that is, Identical Strike Widths.

Strategy (Put Example):

1st Trade Placed Below 2nd Trade:

Buy n OTM Puts ≤ 8 DTE

Sell $2n$ Puts, Higher Strike

Buy n Puts, Higher Strike, Inside 1σ As Shown

2nd Trade Placed Above 1st Trade:

Buy n Puts (May Be ATM or ITM), Inside 1σ As Shown

Sell $2n$ Puts, Higher Strike

Buy n Puts, Higher Strike

Example:

Strategy	Buy/ Sell	Qty	Symbol	Trade Date	Exp. Date	Strike	Type	Price
Double Butterfly	BUY	+1	SPX	08/06/18	08/15/18	$1,625	PUT	−$0.80
	SELL	−2	SPX	08/06/18	08/15/18	$1,650	PUT	$2.78
	BUY	+1	SPX	08/06/18	08/15/18	$1,675	PUT	−$4.80
	BUY	+1	SPX	08/06/18	08/15/18	$1,725	PUT	−$1.60
	SELL	−2	SPX	08/06/18	08/15/18	$1,750	PUT	$0.35
	BUY	+1	SPX	08/06/18	08/15/18	$1,775	PUT	−$0.10

Bias: Neutral * Risk: Low * Reward: Low

Double Long Put Butterfly Risk Profile

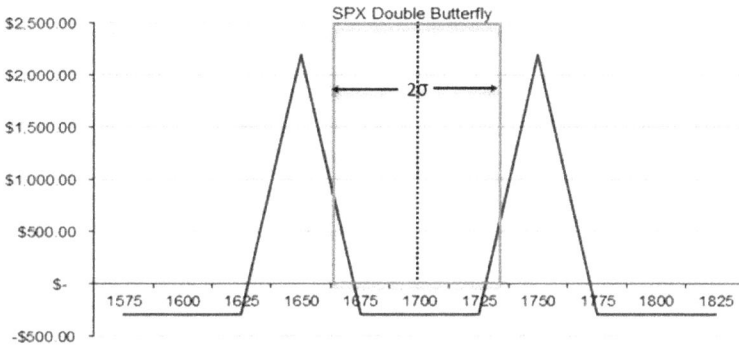

Price Chart: Currently moving sideways; looking for a drop or a rally to benefit one of the butterfly trades

Current IV%: ≈ 50% (Neutral for moderate premium values; avoid either high or low current volatility levels.)

IV Rank: ≈ 50

Trade: Enter two butterfly trades, one above and one below the ATM strike. Notice how the long central options are at strikes within 1 standard deviation (1σ). Also notice how the example uses 25-point strike widths throughout. Because six strikes are used by the double butterfly, it requires two trades.

Typical Strike Deltas:
  Lower Butterfly Upper Long Put ≈ −0.45
  Upper Butterfly Lower Long Put ≈ −0.65
(Notice how both of these long puts are inside 1σ.)

NOTE: Long butterflies that include long wing options and short body options are more popular than short butterfly options. Short call and put butterflies are included for comparison purposes. (See the long call butterfly's note and table for more information.)

Goals: This is a short-term "set and forget" trade that is closed when a profit of 10 to 15 percent is achieved. The profit "zones" cover either a price rally or drop. The winning trade is retained while the losing trade is closed. European-style options are used to prevent assignment prior to expiration.

Manage: Watch for a directional price move in the underlying financial index. Close the losing legs and retain the winning leg(s). For example, the OTM short central strikes might be retained and permitted to expire worthless while the losing long puts are closed to minimize loss. The winning butterfly is retained for profit. Butterfly trades are usually closed several days prior to expiration to avoid *gamma risk*. Butterfly trades are typically closed when they are within 25 percent of the time remaining till contract expiration. Because losses from long butterfly options are limited, occasional losses are considered acceptable.

Profit: Close losing positions and sell the long puts when this trade achieves either breakeven or a profit or suffers a small loss. If the SPX settles at either $1,650 or $1,750, this trade can potentially produce $2,200 in profit.

Loss: This double butterfly can potentially lose $300, as it combines a $200 debit for the bottom butterfly with a $100 debit or the top butterfly. The trader would likely close both butterflies with 3 or 4 days remaining till expiration. **DO NOT PERMIT OPTIONS TO EXPIRE ITM!**

Iron Butterfly

Strategy: Buy *n* OTM Calls, ≤ 14 DTE

Sell *n* ATM Calls, Same Expiry

Sell *n* ATM Puts, Same Expiry

Buy *n* OTM Puts, Same Expiry

Example:

Strategy	Buy/ Sell	Qty	Symbol	Trade Date	Exp. Date	Strike	Type	Price
Iron Butterfly	BUY	+10	QQQ	07/13/17	7/21/17	$142.50	CALL	−$0.47
	SELL	−10	QQQ	07/13/17	7/21/17	$141.00	CALL	$1.16
	SELL	−10	QQQ	07/13/17	7/21/17	$141.00	PUT	$1.09
	BUY	+10	QQQ	07/13/17	7/21/17	$139.00	PUT	−$0.48

Bias: Neutral * Risk: Low * Reward: Low

Iron Butterfly Risk Profile

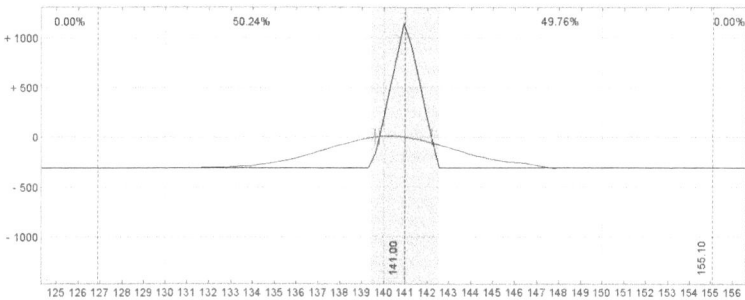

Price Chart: Sustained directional trend; currently basing

Current IV%: ≈ 50%

IV Rank: ≈ 50

Trade: Buy *n* OTM put options; sell *n* ATM put options; buy OTM call options; sell OTM call options, all expire within 7 to 14 days.

Typical Strike Deltas:

Short Calls ≈ −0.50

Long Calls ≈ 0.45

Short Puts ≈ 0.50

Long Puts ≈ −0.45

Goals: Collect premium from the ATM options sold less the OTM options bought. Carefully manage this trade and close it for profit.

Manage: Several option traders enter this trade each Monday and Wednesday using SPX options that expire in 2 days. The trade is often closed for a 10 percent profit within a matter of a few hours following trade entry. Regardless of the financial instrument or time till expiration, monitor the price of the underlying; buy to close the ITM short options and sell the OTM long options as the remaining long option moves deeper ITM and the remaining short option moves farther OTM. Close as soon as an acceptable profit is achieved, which can range from hours to a day.

Profit: Close when this trade returns a profit of 10 to 15 percent.

Loss: Close the two remaining options for a small loss if the price of the underlying reverses direction.

Reverse Iron Butterfly

Strategy: Sell *n* OTM Calls, ≤ 21 DTE

Buy *n* ATM Calls, Same Expiry

Buy *n* ATM Puts, Same Expiry

Sell *n* OTM Puts, Same Expiry

Example:

Strategy	Buy/ Sell	Qty	Symbol	Trade Date	Exp. Date	Strike	Type	Price
Reverse Iron Butterfly	SELL	−10	AAPL	08/25/17	09/15/17	$162.50	CALL	$2.27
	BUY	+10	AAPL	08/25/17	09/15/17	$160.00	CALL	−$3.43
	BUY	+10	AAPL	08/25/17	09/15/17	$160.00	PUT	−$3.28
	SELL	−10	AAPL	08/25/17	09/15/17	$157.50	PUT	$2.25

Bias: Bullish or Bearish * Risk: Low * Reward: High or Low

Reverse Iron Butterfly Risk Profile

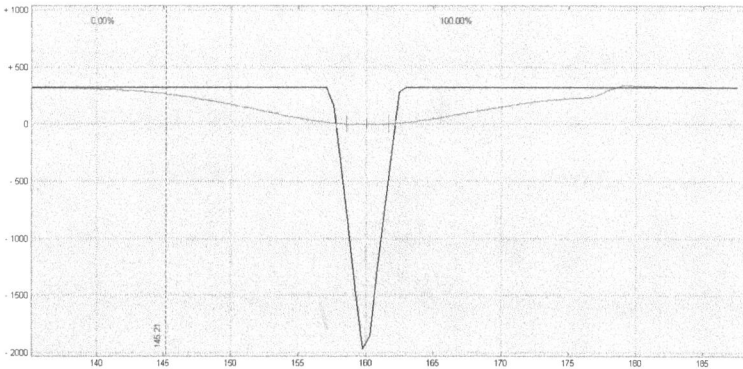

Price Chart: Sustained directional trend; currently basing

Current IV%: ≈ 50%

IV Rank: ≈ 50

Trade: Buy *n* ATM put options; sell *n* OTM put options; buy ATM call options; sell OTM call options, all expire within 7 to 14 days. This is a high-risk, low-reward trade.

Typical Strike Deltas:

Short Calls ≈ −0.45 to −0.40

Long Calls ≈ 0.50

Long Puts ≈ −0.50

Short Puts ≈ 0.45 to 0.40

Goals: Watch for a directional price breakout. Notice how the risk profile shows a $5 price move is required for this trade to return a profit. Close the losing put and call options and keep the long ITM option and short OTM option for profit.

Manage: Monitor the price of the underlying. Buy to close the ITM short options and sell the OTM long options, as the remaining long option moves deeper ITM and the remaining short option moves farther OTM. These modifications change the risk profile and increase the profit potential. Close as soon as an acceptable profit is achieved, which can range from hours to a day.

Profit: Close when this trade returns a profit of 10 to 15 percent.

Loss: Close the two remaining options for a small loss if the price of the underlying reverses direction.

WAITING FOR A DIRECTIONAL PRICE MOVE TO REVERSE IS NOT RECOMMENDED.

Long Call LEAPS
(Long-Term Equity Anticipation Securities)
Strategy: Buy n Calls ≈1+ Year Expiry

Example:

Strategy	Buy/ Sell	Qty	Symbol	Trade Date	Exp. Date	Strike	Type	Price
Long Call Leap	Buy	+5	FB	07/13/17	9/21/18	$165	CALL	−$16.30

Bias: Bullish * Risk: Low * Reward: High

Long Call LEAPS Risk Profile

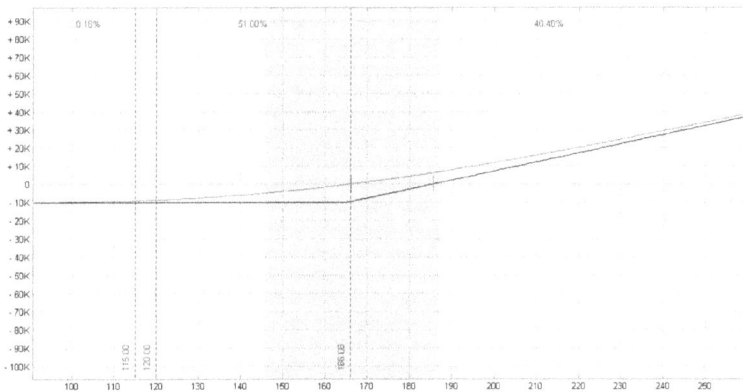

Price Chart: Uptrending

Current IV%: ≤ 20%

IV Rank: ≤ 30

Trade: Buy one or more ATM or slightly OTM call options that expire in 12 or more months.

Typical Strike Delta: ≤ 0.55

Goals: Buy long-term call options on an underlying security that is trending upward. Long options can be purchased for a fraction of the stock price. The return on investment is typically substantially better than a similar trade made on the underlying stock or ETF, even when the security pays a dividend.

Manage: If the long call has returned an acceptable profit and before Theta begins to erode the premium value of the long call options, close them for profit. If deep ITM, determine if exercising the option (receiving the intrinsic value less the remaining extrinsic value) is more profitable than simply selling the long call options for the current premium value. The long call can also be used to cover a series of short OTM call options for additional premium income, which is a common practice.

Profit: Close when this trade returns a profit of 50 percent or more.

Loss: Close this trade if the price of the underlying reverses direction as a result of poor earnings or an unexpected corporate or financial sector event and the premium initially paid approaches a 10 percent reduction in value.

Long Put LEAPS
(Long-Term Equity Anticipation Securities)
Strategy: Buy n Puts, ≈1+ Year DTE

Example:

Strategy	Buy/ Sell	Qty	Symbol	Trade Date	Exp. Date	Strike	Type	Price
Long Put Leap	Buy	+5	DKS	08/28/17	03/16/18	$23	PUT	−$1.60

Bias: Bearish * Risk: Low * Reward: High

Long Put LEAPS Risk Profile

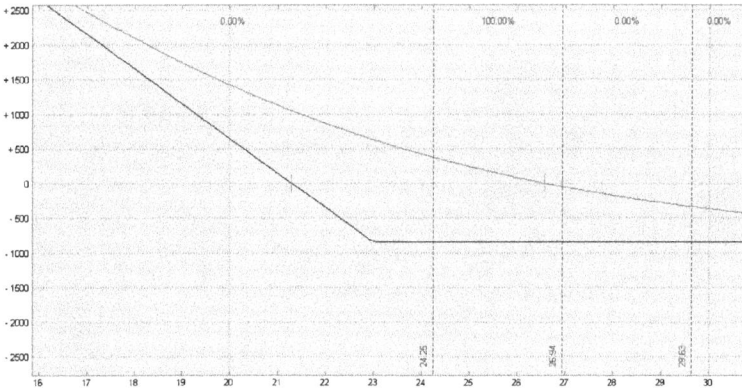

Price Chart: Downtrending

Current IV%: ≤ 25%

IV Rank: ≤ 30

Trade: Buy one or more put options.

Typical Strike Delta: ≥ −0.45 to −0.55

Goals: A strong, sustained drop in the price of the underlying is required to move the long put deeper ITM for a substantial increase in premium value.

Manage: If the long put moves deeper ITM according to the trader's bearish bias (on the basis of the price charts and either corporate or the corresponding financial sector falling from favor), the trader may sell the long puts for substantially more premium than originally paid.

If the long put options move deep ITM, consider exercising the put options when the intrinsic value less the remaining extrinsic value returns more profit than selling the option premium. Also consider selling a series of short-term call options to collect additional premium during the life of the long put. If the price of the underlying begins to rally, sell the long put and consider buying a long call to take advantage of the price increase.

Profit: Close when this trade returns a profit of 50 percent or more.

Loss: Close when this trade approaches a 10 percent loss.

Put Backspread

Strategy: Buy 2n OTM Puts, Typically ≤ 56 DTE

Sell n Puts, Higher Strike, Same Expiry

Example:

Strategy	Buy/ Sell	Qty	Symbol	Trade Date	Exp. Date	Strike	Type	Price
Put	BUY	+10	OLED	8/28/17	12/15/17	$80.00	PUT	−$1.63
Backspread	SELL	−5	OLED	8/28/17	09/15/17	$110.00	PUT	$3.45

Bias: Bearish * Risk: Low * Reward: High

Put Backspread Risk Profile

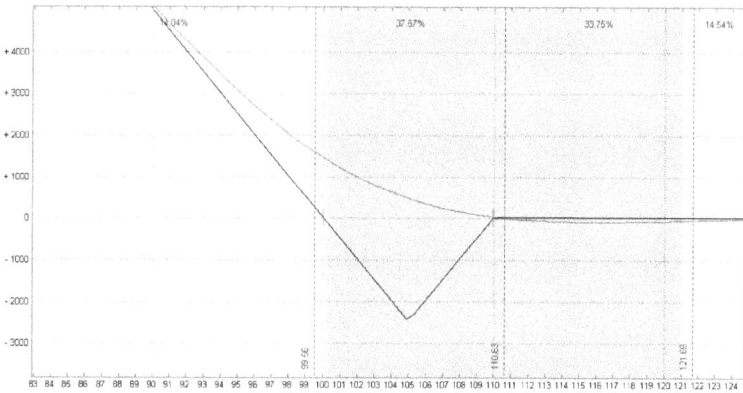

Price Chart: Downtrending

Current IV%: ≤ 25%

IV Rank: ≤ 30

Trade: Sell one or more put options; buy twice as many put options farther OTM.

Typical Strike Deltas:

Short Puts ≈ 0.30 to 0.25

Long Puts ≈ −0.25 to −0.15

Goals: A strong, sustained drop in the price of the underlying is required to move the long put deeper ITM and to achieve a profit in premium value. When the spread width of the strikes is sufficiently narrow, the premium value of the $2n$ long put options increases profit faster than the decline in premium value of the $1n$ short put options.

Manage: If the price of the underlying drops according to the trader's bias, this 2:1 vertical bear put spread moves deeper ITM. The long put premium increases faster than that of the short put's premium. Be prepared to close this trade when it returns a profit of more than 30 percent. If the expected drop in the price of the underlying security and the price bases is followed by a rally, close the trade to avoid losing the profit that may already exist.

Profit: Close when this trade returns a profit of 30 percent or more.

Loss: Close if this trade approaches a 10 percent loss from an unexpected price rally in the underlying security.

Ratio Call Write

Strategy: Sell 2n or 3n ATM Calls, Expire ≤ 56 DTE
Buy or Own n × 100 Shares

Example:

Strategy	Buy/ Sell	Qty	Symbol	Trade Date	Exp. Date	Strike	Type	Price
Ratio Call Write	SELL	−4	EXAS	08/28/17	10/20/17	$42.00	CALL	$2.33
	BUY/ OWN	200	EXAS				STOCK	$41.13

Bias: Bearish * Risk: High * Reward: Low

Ratio Call Write Risk Profile

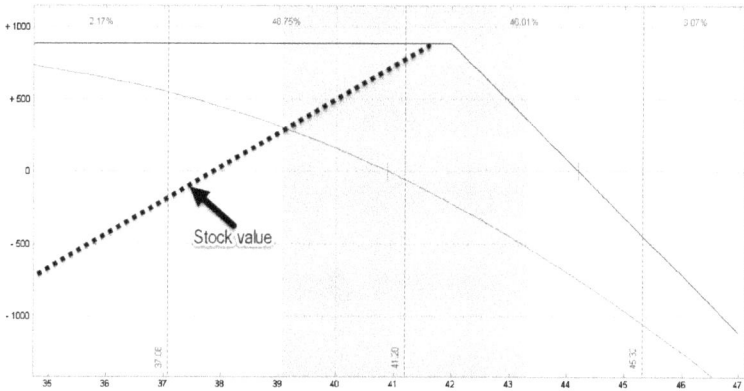

Price Chart: Downtrending

Current IV%: ≥ 40%

IV Rank: ≤ 30

Trade: Sell two or three ATM call options for each 100 shares of stock owned.

Typical Strike Delta:

Short Calls ≈ −0.50

Goals: This bearish premium collection strategy succeeds when the underlying stock drops in value according to the trader's bearish bias. The premium is retained throughout the life of the option contract. The stock's Delta value is 1.0 per share; ATM calls have a Delta of 0.50.

By selling (or *writing*) 2 call options, the short calls partially offset the loss in stock value. Selling $3n$ call options increases the premium collected for additional profit, but also increases risk if the trader's bearish bias is wrong.

Manage: This strategy nets a small return in profit when the price of the underlying stock drops. The strategy is used to both hedge (offset the loss in stock value) and return a profit in premium when the price of the underlying stock declines. If the price of the underlying reverses direction and begins to rally, close the short calls to retain as much premium as possible.

Profit: If the short call options remain OTM, either roll the short calls out and down or let them expire worthless.

Loss: Close if the price of the stock begins to rally and the premium values of the short calls begin to increase in value for a loss.

Ratio Put Write

Strategy: Sell $2n$ ATM Calls, Expire $\leq$ 56 DTE

Short $n \times 100$ Shares

Example:

Strategy	Buy/ Sell	Qty	Symbol	Trade Date	Exp. Date	Strike	Type	Price
Ratio Put Write	SELL	−10	KORS	07/13/17	08/18/17	$32.50	PUT	$1.20
	SHORT	−500	KORS	07/13/17			STOCK	$33.53

Bias: Bullish * Risk: High * Reward: Low

Ratio Put Write Risk Profile

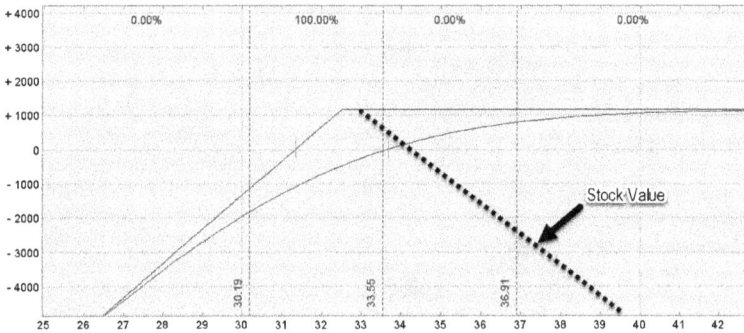

Price Chart: Uptrending

Current IV%: $\geq$ 40%

IV Rank: $\leq$ 30

Trade: Sell two or three ATM put options for each 100 shares of stock owned.

Typical Strike Delta:

Short Puts $\approx$ 0.50

Goals: This is a bullish bias premium collection strategy. If the price of the underlying stock rallies in value, the premium is retained throughout the life of the option contracts. The stock's Delta value is 1.0 per share; ATM calls have a Delta of 0.50. By selling (or *writing*) 2 put options, the short puts partially offset the loss in stock value. Selling $3n$ put options increases the premium collected for additional profit, but also increases risk if the trader's bullish bias is wrong.

Manage: This strategy collects premium by selling put options. It is superior to the ratio call write described previously, because the stock value is increasing rather than dropping, and the premium collected by selling the short puts adds to the increase in stock value. If the price of the underlying reverses direction and begins to drop, close the short calls immediately in order to retain as much premium as possible.

Profit: If the short put options remain OTM, either roll the short puts out and up or let them expire worthless.

Loss: Close if the price of the stock begins to drop and the premium of the short puts begins to increase in value.

Variable Ratio Call Write

Strategy: Sell n ITM Calls, $\leq$ 56 DTE

Sell n OTM Calls, Same Expiry

Buy or Own $n \times$ 100 Shares

Example:

Strategy	Buy/ Sell	Qty	Symbol	Trade Date	Exp. Date	Strike	Type	Price
Variable Ratio Write	SELL	−10	SPY	08/21/17	09/15/17	$243.00	CALL	$2.71
	SELL	−10	SPY	08/21/17	09/15/17	$247.00	CALL	$0.71
	BUY/ OWN	1,000	SPY				STOCK	$244.45

Bias: Bearish * Risk: High * Reward: High

Variable Ratio Call Write Risk Profile

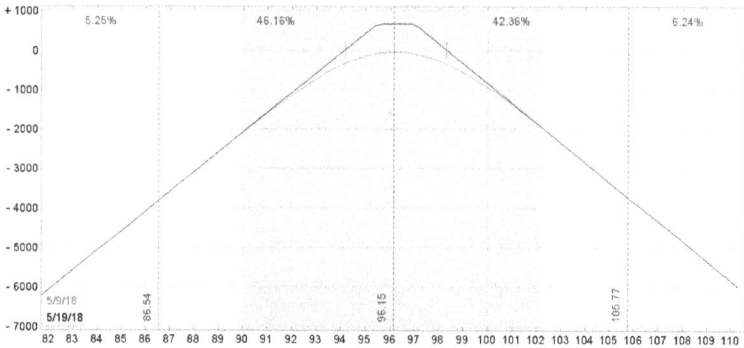

Price Chart: Uptrending

Current IV%: $\geq$ 40%

IV Rank: $\leq$ 30

Trade: Sell an ITM call option and an OTM call option for each 100 shares of stock owned.

Typical Strike Deltas:

OTM Short Calls $\approx$ −0.45 to −0.40

ITM Short Calls $\approx$ −0.55 to −0.60

Goals: This is another premium collection strategy that relies on Theta (the daily passage of time) and the ownership of the underlying stock.

This trade works best when the stock is "stuck" within a narrow price range. If the trade drops below the strike of the ITM short call option, the option premiums can be retained as profit, although the trader suffers a loss from the reduction in stock value.

Manage: This strategy collects premium by selling call options above and below the current stock price. As can be seen in the risk profile, which plots both the stock and option values, this trade has a relatively narrow profit zone comprised of the initial premium collected. The premium is highest when the option strikes remain above and below the price of the stock, that is, the ATM strike. The profit zone can be increased by increasing the strike widths, but this also decreases the amount of premium collected when entered. If the price of the underlying stock rallies and both short call options become ITM, close them immediately unless you are trading a European-style option with ample time remaining till expiration. If the price of the underlying drops and the strikes of both short call options become OTM, either buy to close them for a fraction of the original premium value collected or let them expire worthless.

Profit: If the short call options both remain OTM, either roll the short calls out and down for additional premium or let them expire worthless for a 100 percent profit.

Loss: Close if the price of the stock begins to drop and the premium of the short puts begins to increase in value for a loss. Close both positions to prevent a loss that exceeds 10 to 20 percent.

Long Call Ladder

Strategy: Buy n ITM Calls, ≤ 56 DTE

Sell n ATM Calls, Same Expiry

Sell n OTM Calls, Same Expiry

Example:

Strategy	Buy/ Sell	Qty	Symbol	Trade Date	Exp. Date	Strike	Type	Price
Long Call Ladder	BUY	+5	AAPL	08/29/17	09/22/17	$165.00	CALL	−$2.71
	SELL	−5	AAPL	08/29/17	09/22/17	$170.00	CALL	$1.18
	SELL	−5	AAPL	08/29/17	09/22/17	$175.00	CALL	$0.46

Bias: Bullish * Risk: High * Reward: Low

Long Call Ladder Risk Profile

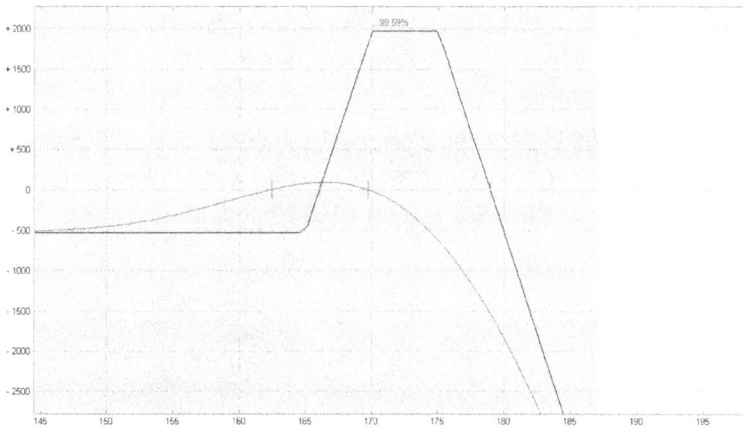

Price Chart: Uptrending

Current IV%: ≥ 40%

IV Rank: ≤ 30

Trade: Buy n ITM call options; sell n ATM call options; sell n OTM call options.

Typical Strike Deltas:

  ITM Long Calls ≈ 0.55 to 0.60

  OTM Short Calls ≈ −0.30 to −0.25

  Farther OTM Short Calls ≈ −0.25 to −0.15

Goals: This is another premium collection strategy that combines a bull call with an additional OTM short call to finance the cost of the long ITM call.

Manage: This strategy includes uncovered short calls, which requires the trader to have the highest option trading level. It is designed to collect premium by buying an ITM call option and selling two call options, one ATM and another OTM. The premium collected from the two short call options must be greater than the premium paid for the ITM call option for this strategy to be viable. The premium collected is shown above the 0 line of the Y axis on this strategy's risk profile. The plotline also shows how a strong price move in either directional can defeat this trade. If the price of the underlying stock rallies and both short call options become ITM, close them immediately. If the price drops, sell the long call for any premium that may remain and keep the short calls as long as they remain OTM.

Profit: If the short call options both become OTM, either roll the short calls out for additional premium or let them expire worthless for a 100 percent profit.

Loss: Close if the price of the stock begins to drop and the premium of the short puts begins to increase in value for a loss. Close both positions to prevent a loss that exceeds 10 to 20 percent.

Short Call Ladder

Strategy: Buy n OTM Calls, ≤ 56 DTE

Buy n ATM Calls, Same Expiry

Sell n ITM Calls, Same Expiry

Example:

Strategy	Buy/ Sell	Qty	Symbol	Trade Date	Exp. Date	Strike	Type	Price
Short Call Ladder	BUY	+5	AAPL	08/29/17	09/15/17	$165.00	CALL	−$2.12
	BUY	+5	AAPL	08/29/17	09/15/17	$162.50	CALL	−$3.25
	SELL	−5	AAPL	08/29/17	09/15/17	$160.00	CALL	$4.65

Bias: Bullish * Risk: Low * Reward: High

Short Call Ladder Risk Profile

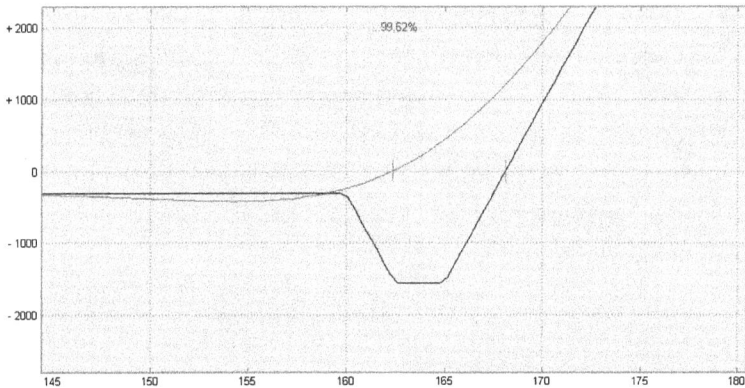

Price Chart: Uptrending

Current IV%: ≥ 40%

IV Rank: ≤ 30

Trade: Sell n ITM call options; buy n ATM call options; buy n OTM call options.

Typical Strike Deltas:

ITM Short Calls ≈ −0.55 to −0.65

ATM Long Calls ≈ 0.45 to 0.40

OTM Long Calls ≈ 0.40 to 0.35

Goals: This is a limited risk, unlimited profit strategy that relies on a strong price rally in the underlying, which places the two long call options deeper ITM. The ITM short calls are sold to offset the initial premium paid for the ATM and OTM long calls. Once satisfied with the profit, the trader will sell the long calls.

Manage: This strategy combines a bear call and a farther OTM long call. It requires a strong price rally to return a profit. The ITM short call is closed when the price of the underlying stock begins to rally according to the trader's bullish bias. The short call could possibly jeopardize this strategy's potential if it is nearing expiration and is assigned. When appropriate, it's important to close the short call to eliminate this risk.

Profit: If the price of the underlying rallies, this strategy can return a profit of 50 percent or more.

Loss: If the price of the underlying remains unchanged, or even worse, drops in value, the premium value of the long call options loses value rapidly as the premium value of the short call options also drops as the options become deeper ITM. This causes the strategy to suffer a net reduction in value that may exceed 20 percent. If the long options are closed while the strike of the short options move OTM and are retained, some of the loss may be offset by letting the short call options either expire worthless or close for less premium than originally received.

Long Put Ladder

Strategy: Buy *n* ITM Puts, ≤ 56 DTE

Sell *n* ATM Puts, Same Expiry

Sell *n* OTM Puts, Same Expiry

Example:

Strategy	Buy/ Sell	Qty	Symbol	Trade Date	Exp. Date	Strike	Type	Price
Long Put Ladder	BUY	+10	QQQ	07/21/18	08/18/17	$145.00	PUT	−$2.60
	SELL	−10	QQQ	07/21/18	08/18/17	$143.00	PUT	$1.73
	SELL	−10	QQQ	07/21/18	08/18/17	$141.00	PUT	$1.15

Bias: Neutral * Risk: High * Reward: Low

Long Put Ladder Risk Profile

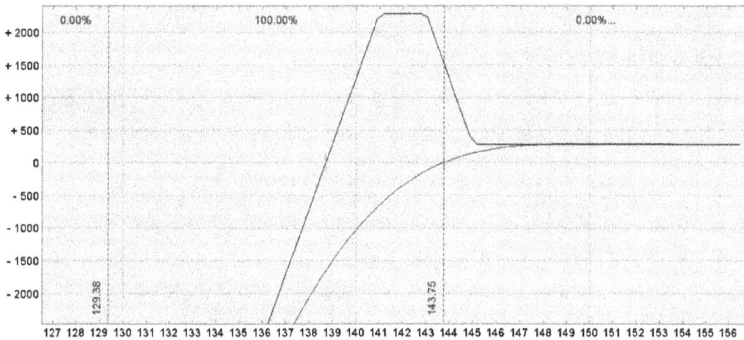

Price Chart: Uptrending

Current IV%: ≥ 40%

IV Rank: ≤ 30

Trade: Buy *n* ITM put options; sell *n* ATM put options; sell *n* OTM put options.

Typical Strike Deltas:

ITM Long Puts ≈ −0.55 to −0.65

ATM Short Puts ≈ 0.50

OTM Short Puts ≈ 0.40 to 0.35

Goals: This is a high-risk, limited profit strategy. The premium received by selling the ATM and OTM put options is more than the premium paid for the ITM long put options.

Manage: This strategy includes a bear put and a farther OTM short put for additional premium collection to offset the cost of the ITM long put. If the price of the underlying rallies, this trade remains profitable. If it remains at its present value, the premium collected when the trade is entered is retained. If the price drops by a small amount, the premium value rises to its maximum value of approximately $2,700. The short puts should be closed if the price of the underlying drops below $139 per share. The premium value of the long puts would simultaneously increase. The long puts should be retained until Theta begins to decrease their premium value, at which time the long puts should be closed.

Profit: If the price of the underlying remains close to its current value or drops by a small amount, this strategy can achieve a profit between $300 and $2,700.

Loss: If the price of the underlying experiences a strong drop and the trade is unmanaged, this strategy can achieve an unlimited loss. This occurs if both strikes of the short options move ITM by several dollars, as shown by the steep negative slope of the risk profile's plotline as the price drops below $139 on the X axis.

Short Put Ladder

Strategy: Sell *n* ITM Puts, ≤ 56 DTE

Buy *n* ATM Puts, Same Expiry

Buy *n* OTM Puts, Same Expiry

Example:

Strategy	Buy/ Sell	Qty	Symbol	Trade Date	Exp. Date	Strike	Type	Price
Short Put Ladder	BUY	+2	AMD	08/21/17	10/13/17	$10.00	PUT	−$2.13
	BUY	+2	AMD	08/21/17	10/13/17	$11.00	PUT	−$0.26
	SELL	−2	AMD	08/21/17	10/13/17	$14.00	PUT	$0.11

Bias: Bullish or Bearish * Risk: Low * Reward: High

Short Put Ladder Risk Profile

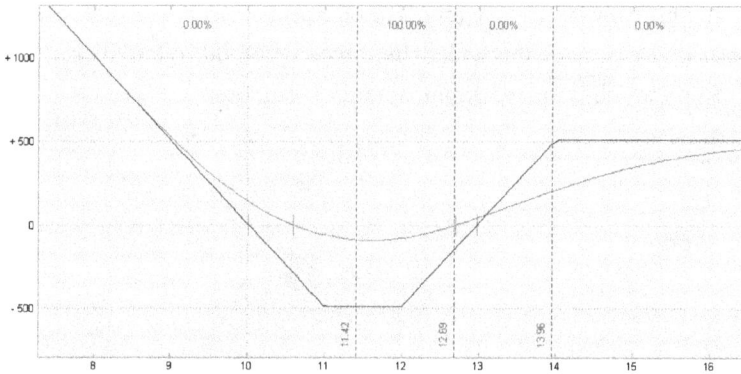

Price Chart: Downtrending Preferred

Current IV%: ≥ 40%

IV Rank: ≤ 30

Trade: Sell *n* ITM put options; buy *n* ATM put options; buy *n* OTM put options.

Typical Strike Deltas:

ITM Short Puts ≈ 0.55 to 0.65

ATM Long Puts ≈ −0.50

OTM Long Puts ≈ −0.40 to −0.35

Goals: This strategy favors a strong downward price move in the underlying security that can return unlimited profit. A rally can also achieve a limited profit. The worst case is when the price of the underlying remains within a narrow range.

Manage: This strategy includes a bull put and a farther OTM long put that adds cost. Selling the ITM puts offsets the premium paid for the two long puts. Carefully watch this trade. If the underlying rallies, sell the calls and keep the short put if it moves OTM. The best case is a strong price drop that moves both of the long puts ITM. If this happens, buy to close the short put to prevent its premium from rising. Keep the long puts until Theta begins to erode their premium values for profit.

Profit: If the price of the underlying rises to $14, which is a 10 percent increase, this trade can achieve a $500 profit. If the price drops substantially below $10, the profit can be substantial. However, this requires an unusually large move for a $12.69 stock.

Loss: If the price of the underlying drops by $1.00, the trade can lose $500, which is the maximum amount it can lose.

Long Box

Strategy: Buy *n* ITM Calls, ≤ 56 DTE

Sell *n* OTM Calls, Same Expiry

Buy *n* ITM Puts, Same Expiry

Sell *n* OTM Puts, Same Expiry

Example:

Strategy	Buy/Sell	Qty	Symbol	Exp. Date	Strike	Type	Price
Long Box	BUY	+5	QQQ	09/29/17	$143.00	CALL	−$2.52
	SELL	−5	QQQ	09/29/17	$146.00	CALL	$0.85
	BUY	+5	QQQ	09/29/17	$146.00	PUT	−$2.82
	SELL	−5	QQQ	09/29/17	$143.00	PUT	$1.48

Bias: Neutral * Risk: Low * Reward: Low

Long Box Risk Profile

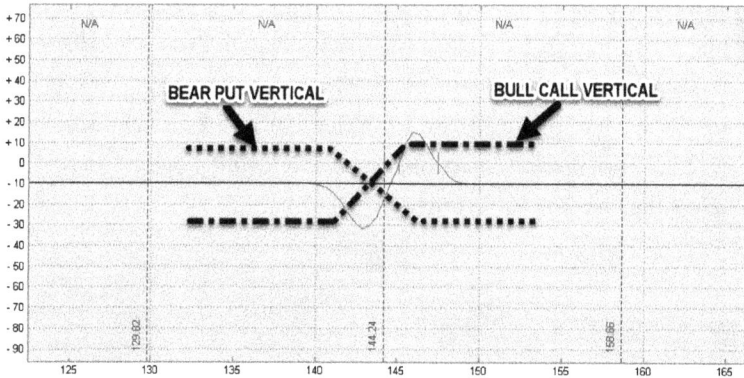

Price Chart: Strong Directional Price Moves

Current IV%: ≈ 50%

IV Rank: ≈ 50

Trade: Buy *n* ITM call options; sell *n* OTM call options; buy *n* ITM put options; sell *n* OTM put options.

Typical Strike Deltas:

   ITM Long Calls ≈ 0.55 to 0.65

   OTM Short Calls ≈ −0.45 to −0.30

ITM Long Puts ≈ −0.55 to −0.65

OTM Short Puts ≈ 0.45 to 0.30

Goals: This strategy benefits from a strong directional price move that favors one of the long options and the opposite short option. For example, a price rally favors the long call and short put, while a price drop favors the long put and the short (uncovered) call. As the strike of a long option moves deeper ITM, the short option moves farther OTM. When adjusted, the resulting risk profile that corresponds to a rally resembles either a synthetic long or synthetic short stock. The risk profile that corresponds to a drop resembles a synthetic short stock.

Manage: This is a bidirectional strategy that requires careful management. The best outcome is a long-term directional price move that is detected early by the trader. Once the losing options are closed, the trader must monitor the price of the underlying to ensure that the directional move continues to benefit the remaining long and short options.

Profit: If the price of the underlying continues a directional rally or drop and the losing long and short options are closed, this trade can return a profit that exceeds 30 percent.

Loss: If the trade is adjusted to accommodate a directional price move and the price reverses direction, close the remaining options to prevent a loss that exceeds 10 percent.

Short Box

Strategy: Sell n ITM Calls, ≤ 56 DTE

Buy n OTM Calls, Same Expiry

Sell n ITM Puts, Same Expiry

Buy n OTM Puts, Same Expiry

Example:

Strategy	Buy/ Sell	Qty	Symbol	Trade Date	Exp. Date	Strike	Type	Price
Short Box	SELL	−5	SPY	09/10/17	09/29/17	$246.00	CALL	$1.96
	BUY	+5	SPY	09/10/17	09/29/17	$248.00	CALL	−$0.83
	SELL	−5	SPY	09/10/17	09/29/17	$248.00	PUT	$3.16
	BUY	+5	SPY	09/10/17	09/29/17	$246.00	PUT	−$2.19

Bias: Neutral * Risk: Low * Reward: Low

Short Box Risk Profile

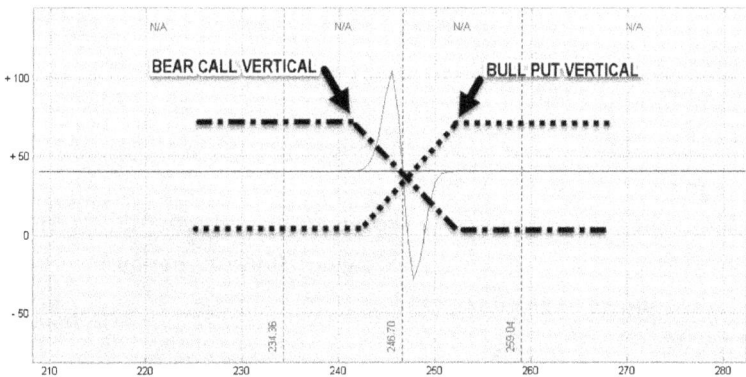

Price Chart: Strong Directional Price Moves

Current IV%: ≈ 50%

IV Rank: ≈ 50

Trade: Buy n OTM call options; sell n ITM call options; buy n OTM put options; sell n ITM put options.

Typical Strike Deltas:

ITM Short Calls ≈ −0.55 to −0.65

OTM Long Calls ≈ 0.45 to 0.30

ITM Short Puts ≈ 0.55 to 0.65

OTM Long Puts ≈ −0.45 to −0.30

Goals: This trade collects premium when traded because of the two short ITM strikes. Looking at the risk profile, the puts form a bull put and the calls form a bear call, although the strikes are much closer to the ATM strike than a conventional bull put or bear call. Like the recently described long box option strategy, this strategy also favors a strong directional price move that benefits one of the long options and the opposite short option. Like the long box strategy, a price rally favors the long call and short put; a price drop benefits the long put and the short (uncovered) call. As the strike of a long option moves deeper ITM, the short option moves farther OTM. When adjusted, the resulting risk profile resembles a synthetic long stock or a synthetic short stock.

Manage: This is a bidirectional strategy that requires careful management. The best outcome is a long-term directional price move that is detected early by the trader. Once the losing options are closed, the trader must monitor the price of the underlying to ensure that the directional move continues to benefit the remaining long and short options.

Profit: If the price of the underlying continues a directional rally or drop and the losing long and short options are closed, this trade can return a profit of 30 percent or more.

Loss: If the trade is adjusted to accommodate a directional price move and the price reverses direction, close the remaining options to prevent a loss of more than 10 percent.

Synthetic Long Stock

Strategy: Buy *n* ATM Calls, ≤ 365 DTE

Sell *n* ATM Puts, Same Expiry

(Longer-term expirations and even LEAPS options are used
to give the long calls ample time to work for more profit.)

Example:

Strategy	Buy/ Sell	Qty	Symbol	Trade Date	Exp. Date	Strike	Type	Price
Synthetic Long Stock	BUY	+5	NVDA	09/03/18	21/06/19	$255.00	CALL	−$33.77
	SELL	−5	NVDA	09/03/18	21/06/19	$255.00	PUT	$31.40

Bias: Bullish * Risk: High * Reward: High

Synthetic Long Stock Risk Profile

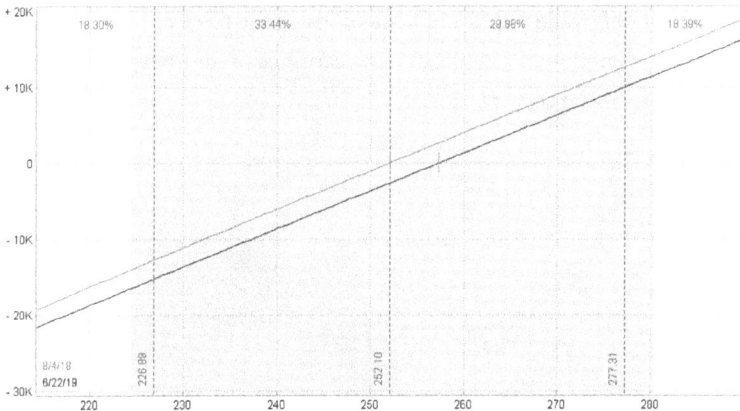

Price Chart: Uptrending

Current IV%: ≤ 20%

IV Rank: ≤ 30

Trade: Buy one or more ATM or slightly OTM call options; sell an equal
number of ATM or slightly OTM put options.

Typical Strike Deltas:

ATM Long Calls ≈ 0.55

ATM Short Calls ≈ 0.50

Goals: Buy one or more call options on an underlying security that is trending upward. Sell a put option to finance the premium paid for the long call option. Provide ample time for the long calls to move ITM for a corresponding increase in premium value. While the premium of the long call options increases, the premium of the short put options decreases in value for added profit.

Manage: When the long call and short put options return an acceptable profit, and before Theta begins to erode the premium value of the long call, close the long calls for profit. If the short puts are far OTM, they may either be closed for much less premium than originally received or permitted to expire worthless. If the long call is ITM, determine if exercising the option (receiving the intrinsic value less the remaining extrinsic value) is more profitable than simply selling the long call options for the current premium value.

Profit: Close when this trade returns a profit greater than 50 percent; long-term expirations can return profits in excess of 100 percent.

Loss: Close this trade to prevent a major loss if the price of the underlying reverses direction as a result of poor earnings or an unexpected corporate or financial sector event.

Synthetic Long Stock Combo

Strategy: Buy *n* ATM Calls, ≤ 365 DTE

Sell *n* ATM Puts, Same Expiry

(Longer-term expirations and even leaps options are used to give the long calls more time to work for more profit.)

Buy *n* OTM Puts ≈ Delta −0.25, Same Expiry

Sell *n* OTM Calls ≈ Delta −0.25, Same Expiry

Example:

Strategy	Buy/ Sell	Qty	Symbol	Trade Date	Exp. Date	Strike	Type	Price
Synthetic Long Stock Combo	BUY	+5	NVDA	09/03/18	21/06/19	$255.00	CALL	−$33.77
	SELL	−5	NVDA	09/03/18	21/06/19	$255.00	PUT	$31.40
	BUY	+5	NVDA	09/03/18	21/06/19	$215.00	PUT	−$15.07
	SELL	−5	NVDA	09/03/18	21/06/19	$330.00	CALL	$9.85

Bias: Bullish * Risk: High * Reward: High

Synthetic Long Stock Combo Risk Profile

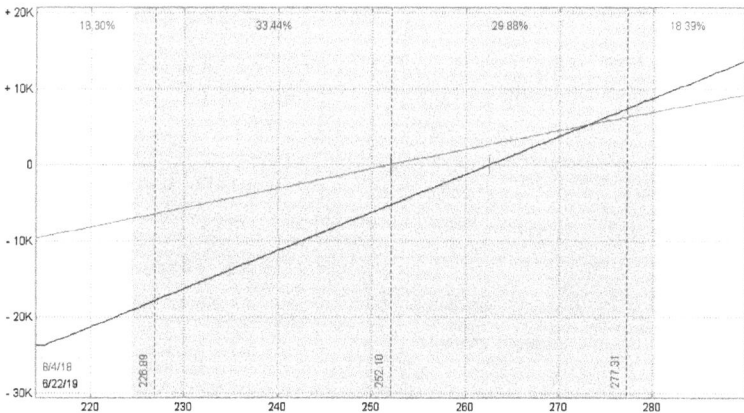

Price Chart: Uptrending

Current IV%: ≤ 20%

IV Rank: ≤ 30

Trade: Buy one or more ATM or slightly OTM call options; sell an equal number of ATM or slightly OTM put options.

Typical Strike Deltas:
  ATM Long Calls ≈ 0.50
  ATM Short Puts ≈ 0.50
  OTM Short Calls ≤ −0.25 (May be closer to the ATM strike)
  OTM Long Puts ≈ −0.25

Goals: Buy one or more call options on an underlying security that is trending upward. Sell a put and buy a put option (a bull put spread) to finance the premium paid for the long call option. Also sell an OTM call for additional premium. If the trade's bullish bias is correct, this strategy can be quite profitable. While the premium of the long call options increases, the premium of the short put options decreases in value for added profit.

Manage: When the long call and short put options return an acceptable profit, and before Theta begins to erode the premium value of the long call, close the long calls for profit. If the price of the underlying drops, buy to close the short call for profit and begin selling a series of OTM short calls that expire in approximately 30 days. If the short puts are far OTM, the bull put options may either be closed for much less premium than originally received or permitted to expire worthless. If the long call is deep ITM, determine if exercising the option (receiving the intrinsic value less the remaining extrinsic value) is more profitable than simply selling the long call options for the current premium value.

Profit: Close when this trade returns a profit greater than 50 percent; long-term expirations can return profits in excess of 100 percent.

Loss: Close this trade to prevent a major loss if the price of the underlying reverses direction as a result of poor earnings or an unexpected corporate or financial sector event.

Synthetic Short Stock

Strategy: Buy *n* ATM or Slightly OTM Puts, ≤ 56 DTE

Sell *n* ATM or Slightly OTM Calls, Same Expiry

Example:

Strategy	Buy/ Sell	Qty	Symbol	Trade Date	Exp. Date	Strike	Type	Price
Synthetic Short Stock	BUY	+5	ADM	07/07/17	08/18/17	$41.00	PUT	−$1.11
	SELL	−5	ADM	07/07/17	08/18/17	$42.00	CALL	$0.73

Bias: Bearish * Risk: High * Reward: High

Synthetic Short Stock Risk Profile

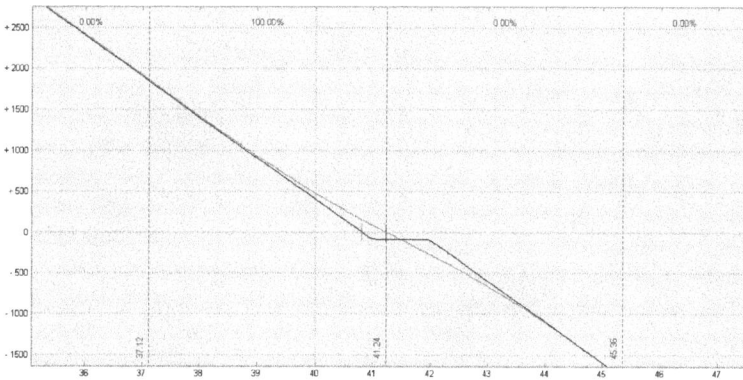

Price Chart: Downtrending

Current IV%: ≤ 20%

IV Rank: ≤ 30

Trade: Buy one or more ATM or slightly OTM put options; sell an equal number of ATM or slightly OTM call options.

Typical Strike Deltas:

ATM Long Puts ≈ −0.50

ATM Short Calls ≈ −0.50

Goals: Buy one or more put options on an underlying security that is trending downward. Sell a call option to finance the premium paid for the long call option. Provide ample time for the long puts to move ITM for a corresponding increase in premium value. While the premium of the long put options increases in value, the premium of the short call options decreases in value or additional profit.

Manage: When the long put and short call options return an acceptable profit, and before Theta begins to erode the premium value of the long puts, close the long puts for profit. If the short calls are far OTM, they may either be sold for much less premium than originally received or permitted to expire worthless. If the long put is ITM by several strikes, determine if exercising the option (receiving the intrinsic value less the remaining extrinsic value) is more profitable than simply selling the long put options for the current premium value.

Profit: Close when this trade returns a profit greater than 50 percent; longer-term expirations can return profits well in excess of 100 percent.

Loss: Close this trade to prevent a major loss if the price of the underlying reverses direction as a result of favorable earnings, a new product announcement, or an unexpected positive corporate or financial sector event.

Synthetic Long Call

Strategy: Buy *n* ATM Puts, Expire ≤ 56 DTE

Buy or Own *n* × 100 Shares

Example:

Strategy	Buy/ Sell	Qty	Symbol	Trade Date	Exp. Date	Strike	Type	Price
Synthetic Long Call	BUY	+5	SPY	08/31/17	09/22/17	$14.00	PUT	−$2.30
	BUY/ OWN	+500	SPY				STOCK	$247.00

Bias: Bullish * Risk: Low * Reward: Low

Synthetic Long Call Risk Profile

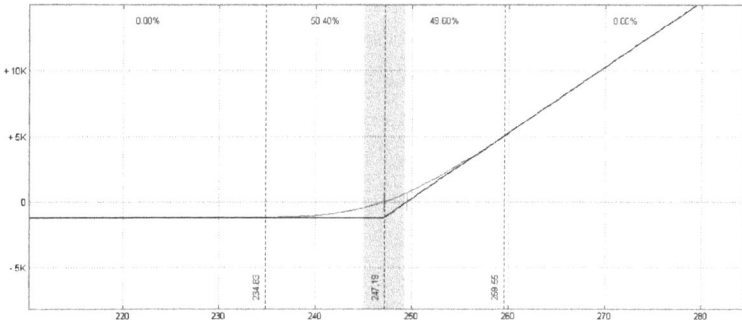

Price Chart: Uptrending

Current IV%: ≤ 20%

IV Rank: ≤ 30

Trade: Buy *n* ATM put option contracts for each 100 shares of stock owned or bought.

Typical Strike Delta:

ATM Long Puts ≈ −0.50 to −0.45

Goals: Traders commonly buy or own stock when they believe the stock price will increase in value. The puts are bought to hedge an unexpected drop in the price of the owned stock. Recall from an earlier discussion, there is no such thing as a perfect hedge. A hedge offsets a portion of a potential loss. As with the synthetic long put options, the 0.50 Delta value of the ATM long calls is one-half the Delta 1.0 value of the stock. The trader expects the price of the stock to rally, as shown on the risk profile.

Manage: When the long stock rallies in value by several dollars per share, the trader may decide to sell it for profit and sell the long puts for the remaining premium. The trader may also consider keeping the stock for use with a series of covered calls. If the price of the stock begins to drop, the trader may decide to sell the stock. A price drop moves the strike of the long puts ITM for an increase in premium value. This offsets roughly half the loss in stock value. If the stock is sold, and the price continues to drop, the long puts may offset a substantial percentage of the loss in stock value. As soon as the premium of the long puts either plateaus or begins to drop from the effect of Theta, the long puts should be sold for the premium that remains.

Profit: Close when the stock returns several dollars per share in profit. If the share price of the stock reverses direction and drops, sell the stock immediately. If the strike of the long puts moves deeper ITM, keep the long puts until the premium either achieves a profit or minimizes the loss from the stock. Then sell the remaining premium either for a profit or to minimize a loss.

Loss: The largest potential for a loss is if the share price of the stock begins a sustained price drop. Note that the long put's premium value will increase as the price of the stock drops. However, the Delta value of each share of stock is 1.00, while the Delta value of an ATM option is 0.50—half that of the stock, itself. Delta increases incrementally as the corresponding option moves deeper ITM.

Synthetic Long Put

Strategy: Buy n ATM Calls, ≤ 56 DTE

Short n × 100 Shares

Example:

Strategy	Buy/ Sell	Qty	Symbol	Trade Date	Exp. Date	Strike	Type	Price
Synthetic Long Put	BUY	+2	EXAS	08/30/17	09/22//17	$14.00	CALL	−$1.58
	SHORT	−200	EXAS	08/30/17			STOCK	$40.78

Bias: Bearish * Risk: Low * Reward: High

Synthetic Long Put Risk Profile

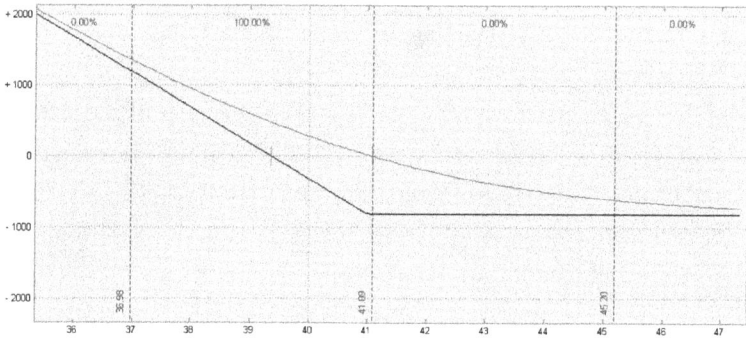

Price Chart: Downtrending

Current IV%: ≤ 20%

IV Rank: ≤ 30

Trade: Buy *n* ATM call option contracts for each 100 shares of short stock.

Typical Strike Delta:

ATM Long Calls ≈ 0.50 to 0.45

Goals: The shorted stock returns a profit as the stock price drops in value. The long call options hedge a loss if the stock rallies in opposition to the trader's bearish bias rather than dropping in value.

Manage: When the short stock drops in value by several dollars per share, the trader places a buy-to-cover order to liquidate the short stock for profit. (Shorting a stock returns a profit from a drop in the price of the stock. If the shorted stock drops by $4.00 per share, the trader issues a buy-to-cover order and closes the short stock position for a $4.00 per share profit less brokerage commissions.) The long call options are simultaneously sold to recover any premium that may remain. If the price of the shorted stock rallies, it is closed to minimize loss; the long call options are retained as they move deeper ITM. These options are sold when an acceptable profit in premium income is achieved, or when the price drop stalls and Theta attacks the remaining premium value.

Profit: Close when the short stock returns several dollars per share in profit. If the share price of the stock reverses direction and rallies, buy to close the shorted shares immediately. If the strike of the long calls moves deeper ITM, keep the long calls until the premium achieves a profit. Then sell the remaining premium either for a profit or to minimize a loss.

Loss: The largest potential for a loss is if the share price of the shorted stock begins to rally. Note that the long call's premium value will drop as the price of the shares of short stock drops. However, the Delta value of each share of stock is 1.00, while the Delta value of an ATM option is 0.50—half that of the stock, itself.

Synthetic Short Call

Strategy: Sell *n* ATM Puts, ≤ 56 DTE

Short *n* × 100 Shares

Example:

Strategy	Buy/ Sell	Qty	Symbol	Trade Date	Exp. Date	Strike	Type	Price
Synthetic Short Stock	SELL	−5	ADM	07/21/17	08/18/17	$42.00	PUT	$1.69
	SHORT	−500	ADM	07/21/17			STOCK	$41.23

Bias: Bearish * Risk: High * Reward: Low

Synthetic Short Call Risk Profile

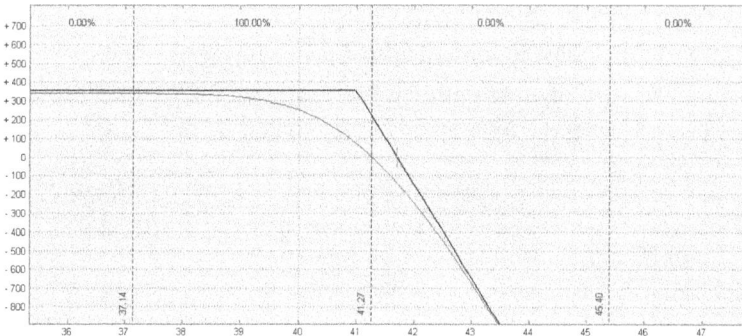

Price Chart: Downtrending

Current IV%: ≤ 20%

IV Rank: ≤ 30

Trade: Sell *n* ATM put option contracts; short *n* × 100 shares of stock.

Typical Strike Delta:

ATM Short Puts ≈ −0.50 to −0.45

Goals: The trader expects a price drop in the underlying security, as shown in this trade's risk profile. As the price drops, the stock initially achieves 2× the premium value lost by the short put options. This difference declines as the short put options move further ITM where the put strikes' Delta values become higher. If the price experiences an unwanted rally, the short puts provide a hedge against the loss in stock value. Recall how a hedge offsets only a portion of a potential loss.

As with the synthetic long put options, the 0.50 Delta value of the ATM short puts is one-half the Delta 1.0 value of the stock.

Manage: When the short stock drops in value by several dollars per share, the trader may decide to sell it for profit and buy to close the short puts to cut off further loss in premium value and to prevent being assigned. If the stock experiences an unexpected (and unwanted) price rally, the trader should buy to cover (close) the short stock trade and keep the short puts as they drop OTM. This offsets a portion of the short stock's loss. After closing the short stock trade, if the price of the stock continues to rally by several dollars, the short put options may even achieve breakeven or a small profit.

Profit: Close the short stock trade and short put options when the short stock and short puts achieve a combined profit approaching 30 percent. (Note that the short puts will return a loss, while the short stock profits in response to the anticipated price drop.)

Loss: If not carefully managed, this trade can potentially lose 50 percent or even more if the stock rallies without trader intervention.

Synthetic Short Put

Strategy: Sell n ATM Calls, $\leq$ 56 DTE

Buy n $\times$ 100 Shares

Example:

Strategy	Buy/ Sell	Qty	Symbol	Trade Date	Exp. Date	Strike	Type	Price
Synthetic Short Put	SELL	−5	ADM	07/07/17	08/04/17	$41.00	CALL	$1.05
	BUY/ OWN	500	ADM				STOCK	$41.24

Bias: Bullish * Risk: High * Reward: Low

Synthetic Short Put Risk Profile

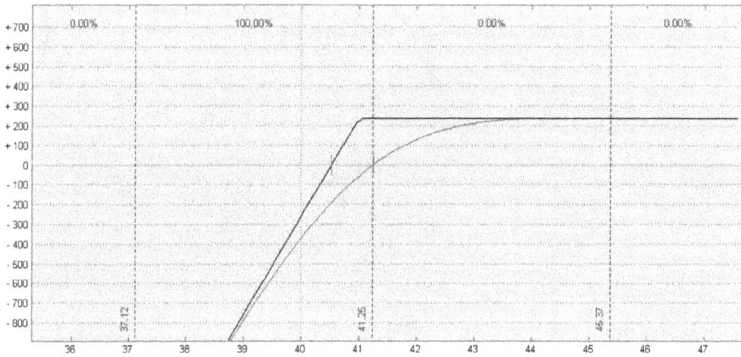

Price Chart: Uptrending

Current IV%: $\leq$ 20%

IV Rank: $\leq$ 30

Trade: Sell n ATM call option contracts; buy/own n $\times$ 100 shares of stock.

Typical Strike Delta:

  ATM Short Calls $\approx$ −0.50 to −0.45

Goals: The trader expects a price rally in the underlying security, as shown in this trade's risk profile. As the price rallies, the stock initially achieves 2$\times$ the premium value lost by the short call options. As the short calls move deeper ITM, the corresponding Delta values increase, which reduces the incremental profit contributed by the uptrending stock.

If the price experiences an unexpected drop, the short calls provide a hedge against the loss in stock value. Initially, the 0.50 Delta value of the ATM short calls is one-half the Delta 1.0 value of the long stock.

Manage: When the short stock rallies in value by several dollars per share, the trader may decide to sell it for profit and buy to close the short puts to cut off further loss and to prevent assignment. Because the return of profit diminishes as the stock rallies, this trade should be closed once it achieves 25 to 30 percent in profit. If the stock is expected to continue its upward trajectory, consider closing the short calls and selling an OTM short call for additional premium.

Profit: Close the short call and sell the stock when 25 to 30 percent profit is achieved. Alternatively, close the short call options, retain the stock, and sell OTM calls (covered calls) for additional income.

Loss: If not carefully managed, this trade can potentially lose 50 percent or even more if the trade is held during a drop in the price of the stock.

Synthetic Short Stock (Split Strikes)

Strategy: Sell n OTM Calls, ≤ 56 DTE

Buy n OTM Puts, Same Expiry

Example:

Strategy	Buy/ Sell	Qty	Symbol	Trade Date	Exp. Date	Strike	Type	Price
Synthetic Short Stock (Split Strikes)	BUY	+5	QQQ	09/01/17	09/29/17	$145	PUT	−$
	SELL	−5	QQQ	09/01/17	09/29/17	$147	CALL	$1.39

Bias: Bearish * Risk: Low * Reward: Moderate

Synthetic Short Stock (Split Strikes) Risk Profile

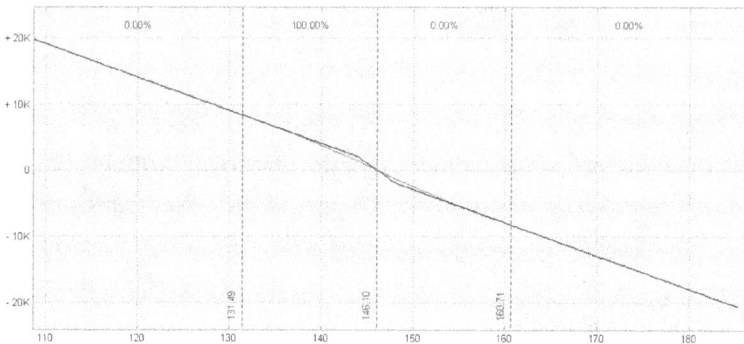

Price Chart: Downtrending

Current IV%: ≥ 40%

IV Rank: ≈ 50

Trade: Sell n OTM call option contracts; buy n OTM put options.

Typical Strike Delta:

   OTM Short Calls ≈ −0.45 to −0.40

   OTM Long Puts ≈ −0.45 to −0.40

Goals: Like the less aggressive version of the synthetic short stock strategy, traders are bearish and expect the price of the underlying security to experience a price drop. This is evident in this trade's risk profile. As the price drops, the premium at the strike of the long puts gains value as the long puts move deeper ITM. The premium of the short calls simultaneously loses value as the calls move farther OTM and can be closed for profit by paying substantially less premium than originally received when initially sold.

Manage: When the short stock drops in value by several dollars per share, watch the P/L value. When this trade achieves a satisfactory profit of 30 percent or more, close both the short put and long call options for profit. If the price of the underlying begins to rally contrary to the trader's bearish bias, the most prudent response is to close the trade. The trader might see how the long puts could be used to leg into a short put butterfly (sell one-half the number of option contracts 1 or 2 strikes above and below). The short calls could be used as the body of a long call butterfly (sell half the number of options 1 or 2 strikes above and below). If the potential return shown by the risk profiles for these two strategies is uncertain, close the entire trade.

Profit: If the trader's bearish bias is confirmed by a price drop, the trade should be closed when a profit of 30 percent or more is achieved, as both the long puts and short calls are simultaneously returning profits.

Loss: If the trader's bearish bias is wrong and the price begins to rally, both the short calls and the long puts will begin to lose value. This is especially punishing if a strong upward breakout occurs. So, this trade can potentially suffer a 50 percent or greater loss. Like the synthetic long and short stock strategies, the trader should be confident that a strong price drop will occur before using this synthetic short stock split strikes strategy.

Long Call Synthetic Straddle

Strategy: Buy 2*n* ATM Calls, ≤ 56 DTE

Short *n* × 100 Shares

Example:

Strategy	Buy/ Sell	Qty	Symbol	Trade Date	Exp. Date	Strike	Type	Price
Long Call Synthetic Straddle	BUY	+2	IWM	09/01/17	10/21/17	$141	CALL	−$3.99
	SHORT	−100	IWM	09/01/17			STOCK	$140.32

Bias: Bearish * Risk: High * Reward: High

Long Call Synthetic Straddle Risk Profile

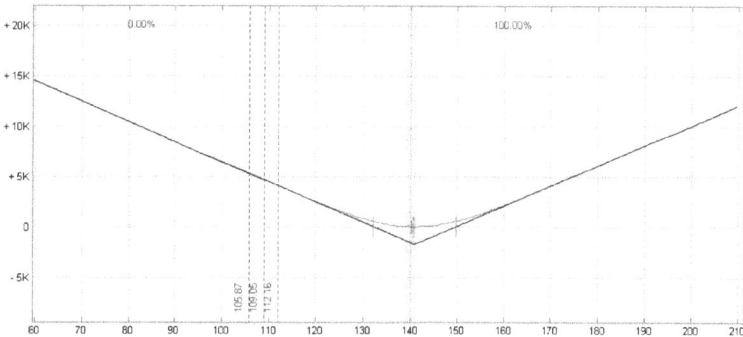

Price Chart: Downtrending

Current IV%: ≥ 40%

IV Rank: ≈ 50

Trade: Buy 2*n* ATM call options, short *n* shares

Typical Strike Delta:

ATM Long Calls ≈ 0.50 (2*n* long call Delta = 1.0)

Goals: This is a less aggressive version of the long straddle option strategy. A price drop rewards the short stock; a price rally rewards the long 2*n* long calls. The net Delta value of this trade is 0 when summing the Delta value of 2*n* ATM long calls, which is 1.0, and the Delta value of the short stock, which is −1.0. The result is a Delta-neutral trade. If the price of the stock rallies, the long call premiums rapidly gain value as they move deeper ITM. If the stock value drops, the short stock increases in value.

Manage: When the short stock drops in value by several dollars per share, watch the overall P/L value. Consider selling the call options to recover as much premium as possible. When the short stock achieves a satisfactory profit of 30 percent or more, close the short stock position with a buy-to-cover order.

Profit: If the trader's bearish bias is confirmed by a price drop, the trade should be closed when a profit of 30 percent or more is achieved. However, this trade has a potential for a much higher return. Retain the profitable short stock or long calls until a price reversal is detected.

Loss: If the trader's bearish bias is wrong and the price begins to rally, the short stock position is closed and the long calls retained. If the underlying moves against the remaining position, exit the trade immediately. This trade is reasonably conservative; when a loss does occur, it is typically quite small.

Short Call Synthetic Straddle

Strategy: Sell 2*n* ATM Calls, ≤ 56 DTE

Buy or Own *n* × 100 Shares

Example:

Strategy	Buy/ Sell	Qty	Symbol	Trade Date	Exp. Date	Strike	Type	Price
Short Call	SELL	−2	BAC	09/01/17	10/31/17	$325	CALL	$0.59
Synthetic Straddle	BUY/ OWN	+100	BAC				STOCK	−$24.16

Bias: Neutral * Risk: High * Reward: Low

Short Call Synthetic Straddle Risk Profile

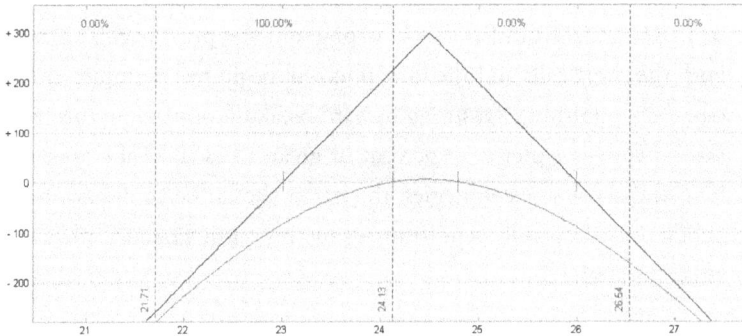

Price Chart: Downtrending

Current IV%: ≥ 40%

IV Rank: ≈ 50

Trade: Sell 2*n* ATM call options; buy/own *n* × 100 shares.

Typical Strike Delta:

   ATM Short Calls ≈ −0.50 (2*n* short call Delta = −1.0)

Goals: This strategy emulates the short straddle option strategy. Like the less aggressive version of the synthetic short stock strategy, traders expect the price of the underlying security to experience a price drop, as shown in this trade's risk profile. As the stock price drops, the short calls move farther OTM. This hedges the long stock's price drop.

Manage: When the stock drops in value by several dollars per share, monitor the trade's P/L value. Because this is essentially a hedging strategy, the short calls can be closed for less premium than originally paid. As with most hedging strategies, they minimize losses rather than being a for-profit strategy. The stock ownership provides additional opportunities. Once the short calls are closed for profit, the stock can be used in a series of covered calls or simply held until the price approaches a support level and reverses direction.

Profit: If the trader's bearish bias is confirmed by a price drop, the trade should be closed when the short call options achieve a profit of 30 percent or more. As mentioned in the previous paragraph, this is a hedging strategy. If the stock price begins to rally, buy to close the short call options and sell the stock when it rallies above the original $24.16 purchase price.

Loss: If the trader's bearish bias is wrong and the price begins to rally, both the short calls and the long puts will begin to lose value. This is especially punishing if a strong upward breakout occurs. So, this trade can potentially suffer a 50 percent or greater loss. Like the synthetic long and short stock strategies, the trader should be confident that a strong price drop will occur before using this synthetic short stock split strikes strategy.

Long Put Synthetic Straddle
Strategy: Buy 2n ATM Puts, ≤ 56 DTE
Buy or Own n × 100 Shares

Example:

Strategy	Buy/ Sell	Qty	Symbol	Trade Date	Exp. Date	Strike	Type	Price
Long Put	BUY	+2	V	09/01/17	12/15/17	$105	PUT	−$4.35
Synthetic Straddle	BUY/ OWN	+100	V				STOCK	103.90

Bias: Neutral * Risk: Low * Reward: High

Long Put Synthetic Straddle Risk Profile

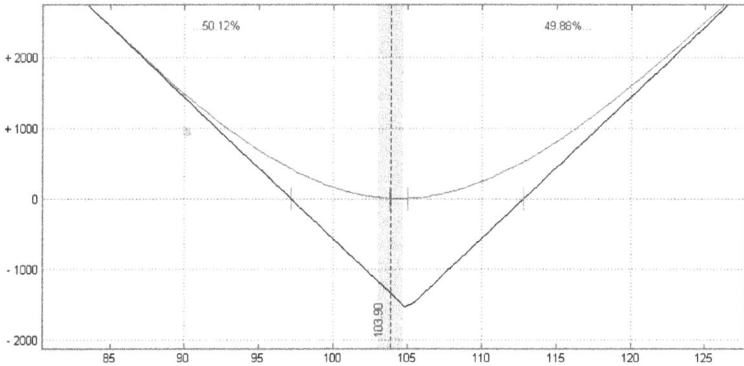

Price Chart: Downtrending

Current IV%: ≥ 40%

IV Rank: ≈ 50

Trade: Buy 2n ATM put options; buy/own n × 100 shares.

Typical Strike Delta:

  ATM Long Puts ≈ −0.50 (2n long put Delta = −1.0)

Goals: As shown by the plotline in this strategy's risk profile, the long put synthetic straddle option strategy resembles a long straddle (buy an ATM call, buy an ATM put). A directional move in the price of the underlying stock returns a profit from either the stock or the two long options, while the opposite side of the strategy is abandoned. Therefore, check the price charts for stocks that typically make strong, week-long directional breakouts.

Manage: Recall how the Delta value of each share of stock is 1.0. The Delta value of two long ATM puts is −1.0. This is another example of a Delta-neutral option strategy. If the stock price drops in value, the stock is sold and the long put options are retained as they move deeper ITM for profit. Theta will begin to erode the premium of the long puts, so be ready to sell them before Theta begins to offset the stock's price rally. Conversely, if the stock price increases in value, the stock is retained and the long puts are sold. Once this adjustment is made, monitor the remaining position and be prepared to close it if a reversal in the stock price occurs. If the stock is kept because of a rally, consider selling OTM call options to create a covered call.

Profit: If a substantial directional price move occurs (either up or down) and the trade is carefully managed, this strategy can quickly return hundreds if not thousands of dollars in profit. This amount is based on the number of shares and option contracts involved in the trade.

Loss: If the price of the underlying stalls and both the stock and the long puts are kept, Theta will begin to reduce the premium value of the long put options. And, of course, if one side of this trade is closed on the basis of a directional move and the price reverses direction, close the remaining position to either retain the position's current profit or prevent what could become a substantial loss.

Short Put Synthetic Straddle

Strategy: Sell 2n ATM Puts, ≤ 56 DTE
Short n × 100 Shares

Example:

Strategy	Buy/ Sell	Qty	Symbol	Trade Date	Exp. Date	Strike	Type	Price
Short Put Synthetic Straddle	SELL	−4	VZ	08/07/17	09/29/17	$48.00	PUT	$0.71
	SHORT	−200	VZ				STOCK	−$47.92

Bias: Bearish * Risk: High * Reward: Low

Short Put Synthetic Straddle Risk Profile

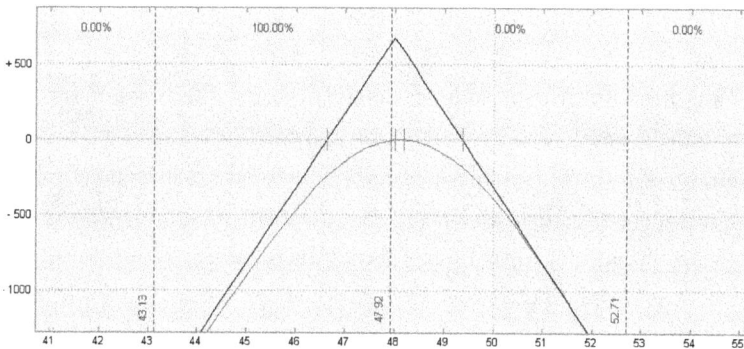

Price Chart: Directional breakout

Current IV%: ≥ 40%

IV Rank: ≈ 50

Trade: Sell 2n ATM put options, short n × 100 shares.

Typical Strike Delta:

  ATM Short Puts ≈ 0.50 (2n short put Delta = 1.0)

Goals: As shown by the plotline in this strategy's risk profile, the short put synthetic straddle option strategy emulates a traditional short straddle (sell an ATM call, sell an ATM put). A directional move in the price of the underlying stock returns a profit from either the short stock or the two short put options, while the opposite side of the strategy is abandoned. Therefore, check the price charts for stocks that typically make strong, directional breakouts.

Manage: Like the long put synthetic strategy, this is also an example of a Delta-neutral option strategy. The net Delta is 0 by adding the -1.0 Delta of the short stock and the two $+0.5$ Deltas of $2n$ short put options. If the stock price drops in value, the stock is retained and the short put options are sold to prevent them from moving ITM for a loss and possible assignment. Conversely, if the stock price increases in value, the stock is sold and the short puts are kept as the premium begins to drop below the amount initially received—one of this strategy's goals. Once the losing side of this trade is closed, carefully monitor the remaining position and be prepared to close it if a reversal in the price of the stock occurs. If the stock is kept because of a drop, consider selling OTM put options below a Delta 0.25 for a few more dollars in premium income.

Profit: If a substantial directional price move occurs (either up or down) and the trade is carefully managed, this strategy can quickly return hundreds if not thousands of dollars in profit. This amount is based on the number of shares and option contracts involved in the trade.

Loss: If the price of the underlying stalls and both the stock and the short puts are kept, Theta will begin to reduce the premium value of the short put options in the trader's favor. And, of course, if one side of this trade is closed on the basis of a directional move and the price reverses direction, close the remaining position to either retain the position's current profit or prevent what could become a substantial loss.

Glossary

Alert. A trader-established notification based on a preset value sent to inform the trader by e-mail and/or text messaging when a specified condition occurs. For example, if the price of the underlying security pierces an established price, the trader receives an alert for either information or in order to take action.

Ask Price. The buying price, or option premium, in dollars and cents, to be paid for each share of the underlying optionable security within an option contract (most often 100 shares per option contract). When trading shares of stock, ask is used to sell and bid is used to buy.

At the money (ATM). An option strike price (or *exercise* price) that is closest to the current price of the underlying optionable security.

Backwardation (or Normal Backwardation). See Contango.

Base or Basing. A term used to describe a sideways movement on a price chart. Rally, base, and drop describe a sequence of upward, sideways, and downward price moves.

Bearish. A negative bias held by a trader who expects a security or market to decline in value.

Bearish Spread. An option spread designed to be profitable if the underlying security declines in price. A common bearish spread consists of buying an in-the-money put and selling an out-of-the money put. This is called a *bear put spread*.

Beta. A measure of how closely the movement of the market price of a stock corresponds to the movement of the financial index to which it belongs. For example, the beta value of AAPL stock is a comparison to its market price volatility to that of the S&P 500 financial index.

Bid Price. Option sell orders are initiated using the Bid cell on the selected strike price row of an option chain. The default price is the Mark, which is midway between the Bid and Ask prices.

Bid-to-Ask Spread. The difference in price between the Bid and Ask values on an option chain. An option chain's Mark value is midway between the Bid and Ask values. Narrow bid-to-ask spreads reflect brisk trading activity and minimize *slippage* in the premium paid or received for a trade.

Bracketed Trade. A trade that includes a limit entry, a protective stop, and a profit target. Typically used when buying shares of stock or exchange-traded funds (ETFs).

Breakout. As applied to market price, a breakout refers to a strong price rally or drop. Traders look for entry opportunities when their analysis signals a possible price breakout.

Brokerage Account. An account held by the client of a brokerage firm that includes securities and cash. The value of the account may be used as collateral (or *margin*) to finance the purchase of stocks, options, futures contracts, and other marketable securities.

Bullish. A positive bias held by a trader who expects a security or market to increase in value.

Bullish Spread. An option spread designed to be profitable if the underlying security rises in price. A common bullish spread consists of buying an at-the-money call and selling an out-of-the money call. This spread is called a *bull call spread.*

Buy-to-Close Order. A buy order placed by an option trader who originally sold one or more option contracts. The buy-to-close order requires the option trader to pay premium to close an active position.

Calendar (or Time Spread). An option spread created by selling one option and buying another on the same security. The option sold expires sooner than the option bought. This spread is named *calendar spread* because the two contracts have different expiration dates. The goal of a calendar spread is to receive more income from the sold option compared with the option that is purchased. If sufficient time remains in the option bought, another option may be sold for additional premium income.

Call. A call option contract entitles the buyer to acquire (or "call away") 100 shares per contract of the underlying security from the seller, who is contractually obligated to deliver the stock to the buyer. Of course, this transaction must occur prior to contract expiration.

Call Option. Option traders buy and sell call options. Call option buyers favor an increase in option values, called *premium*, when the price of the underlying equity increases in market value. This increase permits call option buyers to sell the options for more than originally paid. Call option sellers favor a decrease in premium values, the passage of time, and a drop in trading volatility, all of which reduce premium values. The drop in premium value permits option sellers to close their trade for profit by *buying-to-close* their call options for less than they paid. Call option premium values decline as the price of the underlying equity drops in market value. Equities include stocks, ETFs, financial indexes, or futures contracts. The passage of time decreases the value of options. High trading volatility increases option premium values, while declining volatility decreases option premium values.

Called Away. The buyer of a call option may call the optioned security away from the seller if the option becomes in the money (ITM) by one cent. (See *in the money.*) The seller must deliver the stock to the buyer, who must pay the seller the option price. If the seller does not own the called stock, he or she must purchase and deliver the stock to the buyer for a loss.

Candlestick Chart. A price chart that uses red and green rectangles that resemble the bodies of candles. The candles have lines above and below, called *shadows* or *wicks.* The bottom and top of each candle body represents the opening and closing price for the selected time interval, that is, week, day, hour, and so on. A green candle body represents a rally (a higher closing price than that of the opening price). Red candle bodies represent a drop candle, that is, a lower closing price than the opening price.

Cash Settlement Option. Option contracts on financial indexes are cash settled rather than stock settled. In the case of either a call or a put, the seller must pay the buyer the difference between the option price and the current ITM price.

Chart Interval. Any of several chart time intervals used on price charts. Examples are weekly, daily, hourly, and minute charts. Most traders look across several time intervals to determine the characteristics of price movements across time. Experienced chart analysts use candlestick charts beginning with weekly intervals and working their way to shorter time intervals to develop an understanding of price characteristics. Chart studies are often applied to enhance a trader's expectation relative to future price movements.

Chart Study. A mathematical indicator used on security price charts to show price averages, overbought/oversold conditions, trading volume, average price movements, and much more.

Chicago Board of Exchange (CBOE). The company responsible for providing live options data used by client brokerages throughout the world.

Closeout Date. A predetermined date upon which a contract should be closed to preserve the value that remains within an option position.

Closing Price. The final price at which a security traded at the end of the trading day. When applied to an option contract, this is the premium paid or received when a buy-to-close or sell-to-close transaction is processed.

Closing Purchase. A buy-to-close transaction conducted by the holder of a short option (the option writer) to liquidate an option position.

Closing Sale. A sell-to-close transaction conducted by the holder of a long option (the option buyer) to liquidate an option position.

Contango. This is a term related to a comparison between the spot price of a future and the current contract price. Some option traders borrow and misapply the term, in spite of the fact that options do not have *spot prices*. When the price of an option or futures contract is either rising or falling in value, it is said to be either contango or in normal backwardation. Contango is when the contract price exceeds the expected future spot price. In options, contango implies that the current premium at the strike price of a short position has lost value, profiting the holder of a short option. Normal backwardation relates to the loss in the premium value of a long option.

Contract (or Option Contract). An agreement to relinquish an underlying security if the agreed-upon option price either exceeds the contracted call price by one cent or falls below the contracted put price by one cent. Contracts are managed by The Options Clearing Corporation.

Covered Option. A call option position that is collateralized by a security, such as shares of stock, or a put option contract that is collateralized by cash. When a covered call option contract is exercised by the option buyer, the seller must deliver the optioned securities to the buyer at the agreed-upon option price.

Crossovers. On price charts, a crossover is the point at which one element or line crosses another. This can be the crossover of two moving average plots, a crossover of two study envelope lines, as when a Bollinger band envelope crosses inside the Keltner channel envelope, or when one or more price plots cross a standard moving average plotline.

Day Order. A limit or protective stop order that automatically expires at the end of the trading day. (See *good till canceled* order).

Days Till Expiration (DTE). A popular abbreviation for *days till expiration or days till expiry*. This is the number of days remaining until an option contract expires.

Delta. A mathematical value that determines the change in option premium value resulting from a $1.00 change in the market price of the underlying option security, such as a stock or ETF. Call Delta values are positive and increase from 0.0 to 1.0 as calls drop deeper in the money. Put Deltas are negative and range from 0.0 to –1.0. Put Deltas move closer to –1.0 as the put strike prices increase.

Discount Brokerage. A brokerage that offers unusually low commission and exchange fees.

Distal. A line drawn on a price chart at the bottom of a demand zone near support or the top of a supply zone near resistance to represent the location of a protective stop. Distal lines are the most distant from the current price.

Diversification. An investing strategy that spreads risk across a variety of companies, industry sectors, or both to reduce exposure to a single industry.

Drawing Tools. A toolset contained on most trading platforms that permits the user to draw trend lines, price lines, symbols, text, and other marks on the price chart.

Drop. A term used to describe a downward price movement.

E-mini Future. A futures derivative of a financial index such as the S&P 500 index. The e-mini futures are traded directly in the futures market or indirectly through options on futures. The e-mini financial index symbols are as follows: S&P 500 = ES, NASDAQ = NQ, DJIA = YM, Russell 2000 = TF, and S&P 400 = EMD.

Electronic Communication Exchange Networks (ECNs). ECNs are also called alternative trading networks. The ECNs support stock and currency trading outside the traditional stock exchanges. They are computer-driven networks designed to match limit orders.

Exchange Fees. An options exchange originated fee charged by an option exchange for each option contract bought or sold.

Exchange-Traded Fund (ETF). A security comprised of several stocks or a market index. ETFs are frequently made up of stocks belonging to the same market sector or geographical region. For example, an ETF may bundle several Asia-Pacific or European stocks.

Execution. The completion of a buy or sell order. This is transacted by market makers or, to a lesser extent, on the floor of a stock exchange.

Exercise. Option buyers may execute (or "exercise") their contractual rights when the price of the underlying pierces an option price prior to contract expiration. Call buyers pay the option price for receipt of the optioned security (calls stock away from the seller). Put buyers put stock to the option seller. The underlying optioned securities and cash are transferred between buyer and seller accounts.

Exercise (or Strike) Price. The agreed-upon option price (or strike price) per share of the underlying security. The call buyer pays the call seller, and the put seller pays the put buyer. The underlying optionable security and cash are transferred between buyer and seller accounts.

Expiration Day (or Maturity Date). The final day of an option contract. Once an option contract expires, it is null and void. The goal of an option seller is to have the option contract expire worthless at which time the option can no longer be exercised.

Extrinsic Value. An ITM option's current premium value. When a long option is exercised, its value consists of an option's intrinsic value (the distance from the current price of the underlying security) less the extrinsic value (the option's remaining time value).

Foreign Currency Exchange (Forex). The Forex market is the largest security market in the world, trading in the trillions of dollars every day. Traders speculate on the increase and decrease of one currency, such as the dollar, against another currency, such as the British pound or Euro. They buy currency pairs comprised of a base and a quote currency. Forex buyers buy a base currency against the quote currency if the buyer expects the base currency to increase against the quote currency. If correct, the buyer sells the pair for a profit once the base currency has rallied to his or her satisfaction.

Full-Service Broker. A brokerage firm that provides a full array of products and services. This may include banking, market research, investment counseling, and a variety of investment quality securities. Full-service brokerages usually charge higher transaction fees to cover the higher cost of their services.

Futures Contracts. A contract between a producer and a processor for the production and delivery of a product by the producer to the processor at an agreed-upon contract price. The processor pays the processor in advance of delivery. Each futures contract has an expiration date and must be fulfilled prior to expiration. Futures speculators buy and sell futures contracts with an expectation of making profit margins from the difference between the buying and selling prices.

Gamma. Gamma is an option *Greek*. The value of Gamma controls the sensitivity of Delta to a change in the market price of the underlying optionable security. A 0.15 change in Gamma causes the value of Delta to change by 0.15 with a $1.00 change in the underlying. Experienced option traders are sensitive to the effect of Gamma, particularly near option expiration, where option premiums are most sensitive to changes in the values of Gamma.

Gamma Risk. Since Gamma has a strong influence on option premium values, option traders are sensitive to *gamma risk*. This phenomenon occurs when an option contract approaches expiration at strikes that are at, or close to, the ATM strike.

Good Till Canceled (GTC) Order. A limit or a stop order that remains in force for a sustained period of time. The amount of time a GTC order continues to work depends on the brokerage. Some limit GTC order to 60 or 90 days. Others allow their clients to specify GTC expiration dates.

Greeks. Greek letters used on several of the option chain column headings. The Greeks are found in the formulas used to compute option premium values. Some represent English-language words such as Delta (difference), Rho (rate of interest), Theta (time value), and Vega (volatility). The Greek letter Gamma is used to determine the rate of change in Delta. (Although Vega is not a Greek letter, it was adopted to represent volatility.)

Hedge. A financial position designed to offset losses suffered by the failure of a secondary investment. It can be thought of as insurance against an unlimited loss. A perfect hedge returns 100 percent of the value of a secondary investment in the event it fails to produce the intended results.

Index Option. An option whose underlying security is a stock index. Three popular index option symbols are the SPX (S&P 500), NDX (NASDAQ), and the RUT (Russell 2000), all of which are heavily traded.

In the Money (ITM). A call option is ITM when the market price of the underlying security is greater than the option's strike (exercise) price. A put option is ITM when the market price of the underlying security is less than the put option's strike (exercise) price.

Intrinsic Value. The difference between the current market value of the underlying security that is ITM and an option's strike price. A call that is $5 ITM has an intrinsic value of $5. Intrinsic value applies to the value of the underlying security. *Extrinsic* value applies to an ITM option's current premium value.

Inverted. Used as a maintenance technique to either offset a loss or receive a limited profit when one leg of a short strangle is jeopardized by becoming in the money. Becoming inverted occurs when a trader either buys a put above a short call or buys a call below a short put. The trader's goal is to minimize loss, and in some cases, the inversion may return a small profit. (A short strangle is constructed by selling the same number of option contracts of out-of-the money calls and out-of-the money puts that both expire on the same date.)

IV Rank. Used in place of IV percent by many long-term option traders, IV Rank compares current IV percent to its yearly high and low values. IV Rank values range from 0 percent to 100 percent.

Kappa. An option *Greek* constant used to compare a change in option premium value to a 1 percent change in current option volatility.

Lambda. An option *Greek* used to compare the change in option premium value to a 1 percent change in current option volatility.

Last Sale Price. The final price of an equity security (stock, ETF, option, and so on) when last sold or purchased. (Last is available on option chains to show the last premium amount paid at the strike prices of all call and put options.)

LEAPS. The acronym used for Long-term Equity AnticiPation Securities. LEAPS are typically used with call option contracts in anticipation of a strong price rally over 1 to 3 years. Many option contracts have expiration dates as far out as 3 years.

Legging In. Converting an existing option strategy to another as a maintenance action. Creating ("legging into") a butterfly from a working long call debit spread or a bull put credit spread to either limit risk exposure or achieve profit are two examples.

Leverage, Financial. An investment instrument that provides a higher rate of return using a smaller amount of money.

Limit Order. An order to purchase or sell at a specified price. When buying, the limit order requires the price of the underlying security to be at or below the limit price. When selling, the price of the underlying security must be at or above the specified price. Limit orders are transacted as either DAY or GTC orders.

Limited Risk. A risk management strategy. An example is buying an option contract in which the maximum risk is the premium paid at entry.

Liquid (or Liquidity). The speed in which a security can be traded. In options, a high level of open interest signifies an acceptable level of liquidity.

Listed Options. Actively traded options that are listed on an options exchange, such as the CBOE.

Long Order. Buying a security is said to be taking a long position in that security.

Longer-Term Options. Option contracts with long-term expiration dates, typically those contracts that expire in more than 90 days. Some longer-term options are classified as LEAPS. These expire in 1 year or more. Some option contracts remain active for up to 3 years.

Liquidity and Liquidity Risk. Market liquidity is required for trades to execute in a reasonable amount of time. A low liquidity level indicates a lack of interest on the part of market traders. An illiquid security can languish unbought and unsold for months and years. Traders are advised to avoid entry into low-liquidity securities. Funding liquidity is a concern of corporate treasurers who must find sufficient funds to keep the company afloat, that is, pay bills and make payroll to sustain normal business operations.

Market Depth. The resistance to price change based on trading volume. Market depth is a measure of the trading volume required to move the price of the underlying security. A 100-share trade is not sufficient to impact the price when market depth is high. A trade of 1 million shares typically exceeds the market depth and moves the market price of the underlying security.

Market Order. An order to purchase or sell a security at the current listed market price. The price is established by an authorized *market maker* who represents the security exchange responsible for the selected security. Market orders are executed immediately and have priority over limit orders. Market orders are used with protective stops.

Market Sector. A market category that includes a specific type of business. Categories include basic materials, capital goods, consumer discretionary, consumer staples, energy, financial, health care, technology, telecommunications, transportation, and utilities.

Maturity Date. Also called *contract expiration date*, the maturity date is the final trading day of an option contract. Upon contract expiration, all open positions cease to exist.

Moving Average. A mathematical average of data points over a specified period of time. Moving averages are used on financial price charts to show the average price over a selected interval of time. Examples are the SMA(9), SMA(20), SMA(50), or SMA(200) referring to 9-, 20-, 50-, or 200-period simple moving averages. Other types of moving averages also exist, such as an exponential moving average (EMA) and triangular moving averages (TMA). The EMA places more emphasis on the most recent data points. The TMA places more emphasis on the center data points of the specified range, that is, 9, 20, 50, 200, and so on.

Naked Writing (or *Uncovered Short Puts or Calls*). Selling an uncollateralized call option or a *cash covered* put option. The naked call or put seller does not have a position in the underlying security nor is it *covered* by a long option position as in a bull put spread strategy, which "covers" a farther out-of-the-money (OTM) short call.

Neutral Option Strategy. An option strategy, such as the Gamma-Delta-Neutral spread, used to profit from a small fluctuation in the market price of the underlying stock. Neutral spreads are typically *ratio spreads*. An example is when a number of call option contacts are bought at one strike price and a greater number of call contracts are sold at a higher strike price to achieve Gamma neutrality. The sum of Deltas is used to determine how many shares of the underlying stock must be shorted, where each share of stock has a Delta value of 1.0.

Neutral Spread. An option spread in which the trader believes that the price of the underlying security will move sideways, without either a strong price rally or drop. A common neutral spread consists of simultaneously selling an OTM call and an OTM put to collect premium. This spread is called a *short strangle*. The trader believes that the market price of the underlying security will remain between the strike prices of the call and put through contract expiration.

Novice Trader. An amateur trader who is both uneducated and inexperienced in the dynamics of financial markets. Typically buys high and sells low. Novice traders are rarely familiar with account management or risk management strategies.

Odds Enhancer. Any one of hundreds of mathematical studies used by traders to enhance the statistical probability of their trading success. Odds enhancers are used on charts and tables to indicate such metrics as trader sentiment, trading volume, price breakouts or reductions, and so on.

Open Interest. The number of working option contracts at each *strike price* listed on an option chain.

Opening Price. The first price at which a security or option is traded when the market initially opens.

Option. A derivative of a security that conveys a term-limited contract between a buyer and a seller. The buyer of a call option pays a contract premium for the right to buy call shares of the underlying security from a call seller, that is, to call away shares at the option price. The buyer of a put option pays a contract premium for the right to put shares of the underlying security to the put seller, that is, to put shares to the seller at the option price. However, the option contract can be exercised by the option buyer only if the market price of the underlying security exceeds the option price by at least one cent. This is called being ITM. If the option contract expires before the price of the underlying security becomes ITM, the option contract *expires worthless* and all contract obligations terminate.

Option Chain. A financial table used by option traders to buy and sell call and/ or put option contracts at *strike prices* above, at, and below the current market price of the underlying security. Each option chain has a specific contract expiration date. Columns include essential information such as the Bid (sell) and Ask (buy) prices, current Open Interest, mathematical probabilities, time values, implied volatility, and so on.

Options Clearing. An issuer of tradable option contracts. Examples include the Chicago Board of Exchange, American Stock Exchange, Pacific Stock Exchange, Philadelphia Stock Exchange, International Securities Exchange, and so on.

Options Exchange. A for-profit company that transacts options trades. Examples include the Chicago Board Options Exchange, American Stock Exchange, and International Securities Exchange.

Option Selling (or Option Writing). Clicking the Bid cell of a selected strike price row within an option chain is used to sell (or *write*) one or more option contracts. Most option contracts represent 100 of an underlying security. (See *covered writing, naked writing.*)

Option Spread. An option trading strategy that includes two or more *legs* on the same security at different strike prices. A spread may simultaneously buy a call and sell a farther OTM call (a *bull call spread*). Some option strategies, such as *butterfly* and *iron condor* spreads, include two puts and two calls at different strike prices.

Option Strategy. Any one of many option strategies for buying, selling, or buying and selling option call and/or put contracts.

Order. An offer to buy or sell a financial security, including equities, option or future contracts, or foreign exchange currency pairs. Orders are transmitted by traders to brokerage companies who submit orders to one or more governing securities exchanges. Once received, buy and sell orders are matched by a market maker. Option market makers are contracted by exchanges to fulfill option buy and sell orders. Once orders are matched, electronic records of the order fulfillment are returned to the originating brokerages, who, in turn, notify the trader. Option orders include call and/or put option contracts at one or more strike prices. Some option spreads may also include the purchase of underlying shares of stock.

Order Bar. A horizontal row containing order information including buy and/or sell instructions, number of contracts, option price(s), option expiration date(s), order duration, and order type (limit, market, stop, and so on).

One Cancels Other (OCO). A bracketed order that includes one or more stops. When one stop triggers, all orders that may remain are automatically canceled. For example, when a protective stop is executed, the companion profit target order is simultaneously canceled.

Order Confirmation Dialog. A dialog containing an order description and pricing information on a queued order ready for submission.

Order Duration. Order durations vary with the type of trade required to accomplish the trader's goal. There are DAY (expires at the close of normal trading hours), GTC (good until canceled orders), EXT (remains open during the day's extended trading hours), and GTC_EXT (an extended hours order that is good till canceled).

Order Rules Dialog. A dialog used to establish automated order triggers on the basis of a price, an *option chain* value, or a chart study.

Out of the Money (OTM). A call option strike price that is higher than the market price of the underlying optionable security. A put option strike price is lower than the market price of the underlying optionable security. The value of an OTM option contract is the available premium at the option strike price(s). The premium value, that is, the Mark, is typically midway between an option's Bid and Ask price.

Portfolio Margin. A margin account originally promulgated by the Securities and Exchange Commission. A portfolio margin account grants additional credit to brokerage clients on the basis of a minimum account balance (typically between $100,000 and $125,000) and the client's trading experience. While standard margin accounts are typically granted the use of 50 percent of their account equity, portfolio margin account holders may collateralize up to 85 percent of their account equity. This expands the ability of portfolio margin account holders to extend their trading activity.

Position. The position of a working trade is the number of shares, or option contracts, that are either bought or sold in anticipation of a profit. Option contracts often include two or more *legs* (or *spreads*) comprised of simultaneous buy (long) and sell (short) orders.

Premium. The value of each optioned share of an underlying security at the specified strike price. The premium value is typically midway between the Bid (sell) and Ask (buy) price and is called the Mark (market price). Premium is highest when an option is initially traded. Premium values erode as the underlying option contract approaches the contract expiration date.

Professional Trader. A knowledgeable, experienced trader who makes a full-time living buying and selling securities listed on one or more financial markets is considered a professional trader.

Proximal. A line drawn on a price chart at the top of a demand zone near support or the bottom of a supply zone near resistance to represent a location near the entry point of a trade. Proximal lines are the closest to the current price.

Put. A put option entitles the buyer to *put* the optioned shares of the underlying security to the seller of the *put* option contract if the option price falls below the contract's strike price and becomes ITM. Each option contract typically includes 100 shares of stock. The exceptions are a handful of mini option contracts that include 10 shares per contract.

Put Option. Option traders buy and sell call options. Put option buyers favor a decrease in option values, called *premium*, when the price of the underlying equity decreases in market value. This decrease permits put option buyers to sell the options for more than originally paid. Put option sellers favor an increase in premium values, the passage of time, and a drop in trading volatility, all of which reduce premium values. The drop in premium value permits option sellers to close their trade for profit by *buying-to-close* their put options for less than they paid. Put option premium values increase as the price of the underlying equity drops in market value. Equities include stocks, ETFs, financial indexes, or futures contracts. The passage of time decreases the value of options. High trading volatility increases option premium values, while declining volatility decreases option premium values.

Rally. A term used to describe an upward move in price.

Return if Called. The amount of income received by a covered call writer, expressed as a percentage. The return includes the original premium received when traded, the appreciation in the value of the underlying stock, and any dividends paid prior exercise.

Rho. Rho measures the sensitivity to option premium caused by changes in the prevailing rate of interest. A Rho value of 0.050 causes a decrease in the value of option premiums by 0.050 if interest rates rise by 1.0.

Risk/Reward Management (also Trade Management). The management of a working trade. May be closed for profit or rolled into another option position. The goal of trade management is to either avoid or minimize a financial loss.

Rolling Down. Closing an option and opening another that expires on the same date but at a lower strike price when rolling down puts farther OTM; can also be used to move short calls closer to the money for more premium when the price of the underlying is dropping.

Rolling Out. Simultaneously closing a working option position and opening a new position expiring at a later date.

Rolling Up. Closing an option and opening another that expires on the same date but at a higher strike price when rolling up calls, or at a lower strike price when rolling up puts.

Rolling Out and Up or Down. Simultaneously closing a working option position and opening a new position at a new strike above or below and expiring at a later date.

Scalp or Scalping. The action of taking small profits from a small price increase in a long trade or a small decrease in a short trade. For example, a pattern day trader may buy 100 shares of a stock for $25 per share and then sell it several minutes later for $25.20 per share for a small $20 profit. This requires day traders who scalp throughout every day to use low-commission discount brokerages.

Sell-to-Close Order. A sell order placed by an option trader who originally bought one or more option contracts. If the sell-to-close order is filled, the option trader will receive option premium.

Sentiment (or Market Sentiment). The current prevailing aggressiveness or timidity of buyers and/or sellers toward one or more securities or the financial market as a whole.

Simulated (Paper) Trading. A feature provided on many trading platforms that permits traders to practice their trading skills or to test new trading strategies.

Short Position. Selling a security, such as a stock, option, or future, is said to be shorting that position. Shorting a stock happens when a *bearish* trader sells a stock in anticipation of a drop in the market price of that stock. A *buy-to-cover* order is placed to close the position and take profit from the drop in the price of the stock.

Short-Life Option. A short-life option contract expires within 60 days or less. Many weekly options that expire within days to a few weeks are traded.

Skew. Skew occurs when option premiums become inverted because of a temporary inversion in Implied Volatility values. *Horizontal skew* causes shorter expiration options to have higher premium values than longer expiration options. *Vertical skew* causes farther OTM options to have higher premium values than strikes that exist closer to the money.

Slippage. A change in the premium midpoint that exists between the bid and the ask price of the underlying. Slippage is greatest on illiquid securities which typically have large bid-to-ask spread widths. Slippage is small on actively traded securities having narrow bid-to-ask spreads that are often only a few cents.

Stock Capitalization Categories. Stock categories are divided by *market capitalization*. Large cap stocks are greater than 10 billion dollars. Mid cap stocks range from 1 to 10 billion dollars. Small cap stocks are less than 1 billion dollars.

Stock Scanner. A computer-based tool used to establish specific parameters, such as price ranges, volumes, current volatilities, moving average crossovers, and so on These parameters are used to find and list stocks meeting the established scan criteria.

Straddle. The straddle is an option strategy designed to profit from a strong price move in the underlying security in either direction. Strong trading volatility is desirable. A long straddle includes the simultaneous purchase of a put and a call on the same security having the same strike price and expiration date. A short straddle includes the simultaneous sale of a put and a call at the same strike price and expiration date. Many straddles are traded at the current ATM strike price.

Strangle. The short strangle is a neutral trade strategy that profits from the sale of an equivalent number of put-and-call option contracts on the same underlying security and with the same expiration dates. The strike prices are far OTM to avoid exercise throughout the option contract life. The goal of the short strangle is to collect premium by selling one or more put-and-call contracts. The long strangle buys put-and-call contracts at different strike prices that expire on the same contract date. The buyer of a long strangle seeks a strong movement in the price of the underlying security.

With a substantial move in the underlying, the profitable position can be sold for more premium than originally spent on both legs of the strangle option.

Strike Price. Strike prices are in a column at the center of an option chain. An ATM strike price is closest to the market value of the underlying security. OTM call strike prices are greater than the ATM strike price; OTM put strike prices are lower than the ATM strike price. Option traders evaluate premium, open interest, and other values at different strike prices when constructing an option strategy. An option's strike price is also referred to as *the exercise price*.

Tau. The absolute change in option price in response to a 1.0 percent change in volatility. Tau is also used to capture the sensitivity of an option's premium to a change in implied volatility.

Target Exit Point. A predetermined price to close a working order. The trader (1) buys an option contract for less than paid at entry, or (2) sells an option contract for more than paid at entry. (Buy for a dime and sell to close for a dollar, or sell for a dollar and buy to close for a dime.)

Time Premium. The reduction of an option's premium value, measured by the Greek Theta, caused by the passage of time. The decay of time premium is also referred to as *extrinsic value*. Premium value declines more rapidly as an option contract approaches the contract expiration date.

Time Spread. An option spread consisting of the purchase of an option and the simultaneous sale of a *different* option on the *same* security with a *nearer* expiration date. The purpose of a time spread is to profit from the accelerated loss in time value of the option that is written, relative to the option that is purchased. Time spreading is often a *neutral* strategy, but it can also be bullish or bearish, depending upon the options involved (more often referred to as a *calendar spread*).

Trading Days. There are 252 trading days in the year. (Also see trading hours.)

Trading Floor. The main floor of a stock or options exchange where market makers fill sell and buy orders. Most trading floor activity is being replaced by automated, computer-based trading.

Trading Hours. Normal trading hours begin at 9:30 a.m. and close at 4:00 p.m. EST. Morning extended trading hours are from 4:00 a.m. till 9:30 a.m. EST. Evening extended trading hours are from 4:00 p.m. through 8:00 p.m. EST.

Trading Ladder. A trading interface on a computer with vertical green and red bars that look like ladders. Each bar represents a price point of the underlying security. Clicking a green bar is used to buy a security at the selected price; clicking a red bar is used to sell a security at the selected price. Multiple OCO-style orders with a limit buy order, a protective stop, and a profit target (a *bracketed order*) are often structured and sent on trading ladders. Trading ladders are popular for use by pattern day traders and futures speculators.

Trading Platform. A trading platform is a computer-based trading application, either installed directly on a brokerage client's computer or accessible through the Internet. Trading platforms provide an interface between a brokerage client and the brokerage for round trip order entry, processing, and confirmation.

Transaction Fees (Commissions and Exchange Fees). The cost of buying or selling a security. Commissions and exchange fees are charged by brokerage firms. The commissions paid are typically governed by a brokerage schedule. They can be a fixed fee per equity trade, such as $6.99 or $9.99 per trade or a per-share fee, such as $0.005 per share. Exchange fees originate at the options exchange, such as the CBOE. An exchange fee is charged for each option contract traded, and can range from $0.50 per contract to $1.50 per contract. Financial index option exchange fees are among the highest exchange fees charged to brokerages, which pass exchange fees through to their client transactions. Exchange fees are paid round trip, that is, upon both trade entry and exit.

Trend Line. Trend lines are used on price charts to show price direction. An upward trend line is called a *rally*, a downward trend line is called a *drop*. A sideways trend line is said to be *basing*. If a price is making a series of higher highs and higher lows, the price is said to be in an uptrend. If making a series of lower lows and lower highs, it is said to be in a downtrend.

Truncated Risk. Risk can be *truncated* (or hedged) by entering a stop-loss or buying/selling a position to limit possible losses of a working position. When an option contract is purchased, it has limited risk and unlimited reward. The risk is the money originally spent on option premium. Unlimited reward is based on a movement in the underlying in the trader's favor. For example, buying a call that moves deep ITM can produce a profit that is many times greater than the original premium paid when the trade was entered.

Underlying. A stock, ETF, financial index, or futures contract. Option contracts are financial derivatives of an *underlying* security. This term is commonly used by traders who buy and sell equities, futures, and Forex pairs.

Vega. Vega reflects a change in an option's price resulting from a change in the underlying security's *implied volatility*. Vega causes a change in premium value for every 1 percent change in implied volatility. A Vega value of 0.10 causes a premium change of $0.10 for each 1 percent change in implied volatility.

Vertical Spread. An option strategy comprised of two call or two put positions, one above the other, that is, arranged vertically. A *bull call spread* is an example that includes buying a call and selling a call above, that is, at a higher strike price. A *bear put spread* includes buying a put and selling a put below, that is, at a lower strike price.

Volatility. A measure of the frequency at which trading is occurring; also a measure of trader sentiment. High current volatility indicates higher than usual trading activity. Historical volatility for a specific security is the average number of daily trades conducted over the past 12 months. Implied volatility compares current trading volume to historical volatility. Options traders make extensive use of implied volatility data. Volatility can have the most impact on the time value of option premium. High volatility causes greater price fluctuation, increasing risk and corresponding option premiums, and is most noticeable for at-the-money options.

Volume. For options, the number of contracts that have been traded within a specific time period, usually a day or a week. For equity securities, futures, and Forex, the volume represents the number of trades, typically in the millions, that are traded during each trading day.

VWAP. VWAP stands for *volume-weighted average price*. The VWAP is a measure of the underlying's price based upon the number of shares or contracts traded at different prices. It is the weighted average price at which most of the trading has occurred.

Watch List. A table that lists tradable securities of interest to a trader, usually stocks, ETFs, and futures. Many traders have multiple watch lists that fall into different categories or market sectors.

Zeta. A rarely used option *Greek* constant that measures the sensitivity of an option price to volatility.

About the Author

Russell A. Stultz has been writing technology, management, and investment books for several years, many distributed in 18 languages. This is his 59th book and third options book. The second edition of his highly successful *The Only Options Book You'll Ever Need* will be released in early 2019.

Stultz worked in the electronics industry including Dallas-based Texas Instruments Incorporated while attending St. Petersburg Junior College, the University of Texas at Arlington, and the University of Texas at Austin. While at TI, he worked as a technical writer, instructional designer, and manager. He wrote several management and technology books for Prentice-Hall, Inc.'s college textbook and trade divisions. He founded Wordware Publishing, Inc., a successful three-division, fully staffed book and software publishing company, and served as Wordware's CEO for 27 years. Wordware was sold in 2009. Russell took formal trading courses from the Online Trading Academy and TD Ameritrade's Investools educational division. He became a full-time market trader specializing in options and futures. He founded the 450-member North Texas Investment Strategies Club to network with other regional market traders.

Index

OTHER TITLES FROM THE ECONOMICS AND PUBLIC POLICY COLLECTION

Philip Romero, The University of Oregon and
Jeffrey Edwards, North Carolina A&T State University, *Editors*

- *A Primer on Microeconomics, Second Edition, Volume II: Competition and Constraints*
  by Thomas M. Beveridge
- *A Primer on Microeconomics, Second Edition, Volume I: Fundamentals of Exchange*
  by Thomas M. Beveridge
- *A Primer on Macroeconomics, Second Edition, Volume II: Policies and Perspectives*
  by Thomas M. Beveridge
- *A Primer on Macroeconomics, Second Edition, Volume I: Elements and Principles*
  by Thomas M. Beveridge
- *Macroeconomics, Second Edition, Volume I* by David G. Tuerck
- *Macroeconomics, Second Edition, Volume II* by David G. Tuerck
- *Economic Renaissance In the Age of Artificial Intelligence* by Apek Mulay
- *Disaster Risk Management: Case Studies in South Asian Countries*
  by Huong Ha, R. Lalitha S. Fernando, and Sanjeev Kumar Mahajan

Announcing the Business Expert Press Digital Library

Concise e-books business students need for classroom and research

This book can also be purchased in an e-book collection by your library as

- *a one-time purchase,*
- *that is owned forever,*
- *allows for simultaneous readers,*
- *has no restrictions on printing, and*
- *can be downloaded as PDFs from within the library community.*

Our digital library collections are a great solution to beat the rising cost of textbooks. E-books can be loaded into their course management systems or onto students' e-book readers.
The **Business Expert Press** digital libraries are very affordable, with no obligation to buy in future years. For more information, please visit **www.businessexpertpress.com/librarians**. To set up a trial in the United States, please email **sales@businessexpertpress.com**.

www.ingramcontent.com/pod-product-compliance
Lightning Source LLC
Chambersburg PA
CBHW061221220326
41599CB00025B/4715